...ence Guide
to Handbooks
and Annuals

(1994 edition)

**Volumes I-X and
'72-'94 Annuals**

J. William Pfeiffer, Ph.D., J.D.

Amsterdam • Johannesburg • Oxford
San Diego • Sydney • Toronto

Amsterdam
Pfeiffer & Company
Roggestraat 15
2153 GC Nieuw-Vennep
The Netherlands
31-2526-89840, FAX 31-2526-86885

San Diego
Pfeiffer & Company
8517 Production Avenue
San Diego, California 92121
United States of America
(619) 578-5900; FAX (619) 578-2042

Johannesburg
Pfeiffer & Company
P.O. Box 4684, Randburg, 2125
9 Langwa Street, Strijdom Park, Randburg, 2194
Republic of South Africa
27-11-792-8465/6/7, FAX 27-11-792-8046

Sydney
Pfeiffer & Company
6/1 Short Street
Chatswood NSW 2067
Australia
61-2-417-5551, FAX 61-2-417-5621

Oxford
Pfeiffer & Company
27 Hanborough Business Park, Lodge Road
Long Hanborough, Witney
Oxfordshire OX8 8LH
England
44-99-388-3994, FAX 44-99-388-3996

Toronto
Pfeiffer & Company
4190 Fairview Street
Burlington, Ontario L7L 4Y8
Canada
1-416-632-5832, FAX 1-416-333-5675

TABLE OF CONTENTS

INVENTORIES, QUESTIONNAIRES, AND SURVEYS

INTRODUCTION

J. William Pfeiffer

The *Reference Guide to Handbooks and Annuals* is intended for use by practitioners of human resource development. It serves as an index to the materials in the ten volumes of *A Handbook of Structured Experiences for Human Relations Training* and the twenty-three volumes of our *Annuals*. In each section the titles are first organized into appropriate categories according to subject area and then, within each category, listed in order of their publication date. Following these three sections are name and title indices.

This edition of the *Reference Guide* reflects a change in how we refer to materials. The term "structured experiences" has been replaced with "experiential learning activities"; the term "instruments" has been replaced with "inventories, questionnaires, and surveys"; and the terms "lecturettes," "theory and practice papers," "resources," and "professional development papers" have been replaced with "presentation and discussion resources." The new titles are more descriptive of the contents of the sections and allow greater flexibility in meeting the needs and interests of practitioners.

In addition, each of the new sections now offers a simpler system of categorization than the one we used previously. The new categories are Individual Development, Communication, Problem Solving, Groups, Teams, Consulting, Facilitating, and Leadership. Each category is further divided into logical subcategories.

CLASSIFICATION OF DESIGN COMPONENTS

The chart entitled "The Technology of Human Relations Training"[1] illustrates the relationship between learner involvement and the locus of

---

[1] Based in part on *The Awareness Model: A Rationale of Learning and Its Application to Individual and Organizational Practices,* by J. Hall, 1971, Plano, TX: Teleometrics; and on "How to Choose a Leadership Pattern" by R. Tannenbaum and W.H. Schmidt, *Harvard Business Review,* May-June 1973, pp. 162-164, 166-168.

The Technology of Human Relations Training

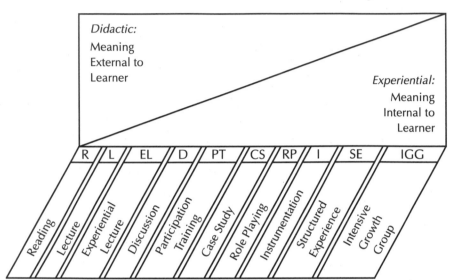

Low Involvement. . . . . High Involvement

Didactic:
Meaning
External to
Learner

Experiential:
Meaning
Internal to
Learner

| R | L | EL | D | PT | CS | RP | I | SE | IGG |

Reading — Lecture — Experiential Lecture — Discussion — Participation Training — Case Study — Role Playing — Instrumentation — Structured Experience — Intensive Growth Group

meaning in training. With *experiential* approaches—those that primarily stress active participant involvement versus passive receptivity—the learning is presumably internalized more effectively.

Reading along the bottom of the chart, we see a classification of training design components, ordered according to the extent to which they incorporate learner involvement. The least involving intervention is reading, in which the learners are in a reactive mode, passively receiving and vicariously experiencing. The most involving intervention is the intensive growth group, in which the learners are encouraged to be *proactive* to take responsibility for their own learning. In between these two extremes are activities that range from lectures to structured experiences.

The experiential lecture is more involving than the traditional lecture because it incorporates activities on the part of the "audience." Interspersed among the sections of content are brief interactions among participants. These interruptions are designed either to personalize the points of the lecture and/or to generate readiness for the next topic.

Discussion is a time-honored teaching intervention that has been extended and refined in participation training. The case-study method, popular in business education, is closely related to role playing, in which a "case" is acted out in a semistructured format.

In instrumentation, which involves learners in self-assessment, the didactic component comes from the theory underlying the items of the scale. Structured experiences stress high participation and "processing" of data generated during interactive activities.

Intensive growth groups exist in many forms, such as counseling, T-groups, encounter, and therapy. They are characterized by high learner involvement and interaction. The data for learning come from the life experiences and here-and-now reactions of the members. Participants are expected to integrate their learning into new self-concepts on their own terms.

The involvement continuum in the chart can be seen in the same relationship to other dimensions, such as risk, self-disclosure, and interaction. Each design component is useful for a different purpose, and there are training situations in which each would be appropriate.

Facilitators are continually faced with the task of planning activities to meet the learning needs of participants. The design problem can be represented graphically as follows:

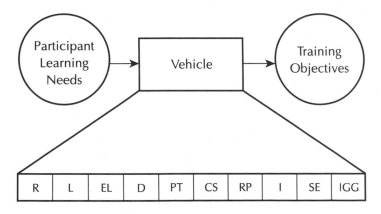

The choice of an effective intervention is made after an assessment of the learning needs of participants and a statement of training objectives. The maturity of the group, the skill of the facilitator, and the environment in which training takes place determine which approach is used.

AN EXPERIENTIAL MODEL

Experiential learning occurs when a person engages in some activity, looks back at the activity critically, abstracts some useful insight from the analysis, and puts the result to work. Of course, this process is experienced spontaneously in everyone's ordinary living. We call it an *inductive* process: proceeding from observation rather than from a priori "truth" (as in the *deductive* process). A *structured* experience provides a framework in which the inductive process can be facilitated. Each experiential learning activity follows the steps of a theoretical cycle.

The Experiential Learning Cycle

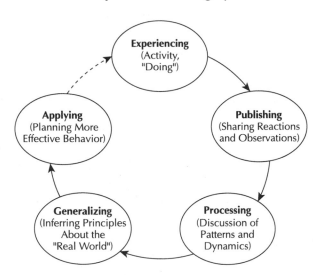

Experiencing

The initial stage is the data-generating part of the experiential learning activity. It is the step .that is often associated with "games" or fun. Obviously, if the process stops after this stage, all learning is left to chance, and the facilitator has not completed the task. Almost any activity that involves either self-assessment or interpersonal interaction can be used as the "doing" part of experiential learning. The following are common individual and group activities:

- Making products or models
- Creating art objects
- Writing
- Role playing
- Problem solving or sharing information
- Giving and receiving feedback
- Self-disclosure
- Fantasy
- Communicating verbally or nonverbally
- Analyzing case material
- Planning
- Competing or collaborating

These activities can be carried out by individuals, pairs, trios, small groups, group-on-group arrangements,[2] or large groups. The learning objectives would dictate both the activity and the appropriate groupings.

It is important to note that the objectives of experiential learning activities are necessarily general and are stated in terms such as "to explore...," "to examine...," "to study...," "to identify...," etc. Inductive learning means learning through discovery, and the exact things to be learned cannot be specified beforehand. All that is wanted in this stage of the learning cycle is to develop a common data base for the discussion that follows. This means that whatever happens in the activity, whether expected or not, becomes the basis for critical analysis; participants may learn serendipitously.

---

[2] A group-on-group configuration consists of two groups of participants. One group forms a circle and actively participates in an activity; the other group forms a circle around the first group and observes the first group's activities.

Sometimes facilitators spend an inordinate amount of energy planning the activity but leave the examination of it unplanned. As a consequence, learning may not be facilitated. The next four steps of the experiential learning cycle are even more important than the experiencing phase. Accordingly, the facilitator needs to be careful that the activity does not generate excess data or create an atmosphere that makes discussion of the results difficult. There can be a lot of excitement and "fun" as well as conflict in human interaction, but these are not synonymous with learning; they provide the common references for group inquiry.

Publishing

The second stage of the cycle is roughly analogous in data-processing terms to inputting data. People have experienced an activity and now they presumably are ready to share what they saw and/or how they felt during the event. This step involves finding out what happened within individuals, at both cognitive and affective levels, while the activity was progressing and making that information available to the group. A number of methods help to facilitate the publishing, or declaring, of the reactions and observations of individual participants, including the following:

- Recording data during the experiencing stage (putting data aside for later discussion): ratings of such things as productivity, satisfaction, confidence, communication, etc.; adjectives capturing feelings at various points.

- Whips: quick free-association go-arounds on various topics concerning the activity.

- Subgroup sharing: generating lists such as the double-entry one of "What we saw/how we felt."

- Posting/round-robin listing: total-group input recorded on newsprint flip chart.

- Ratings: developing ratings of relevant dimensions of the activity, tallying and averaging these measures.

- Go-around: systematic "interviewing" of individuals about their experiences during the activity.

- Nominations: variation of the "Guess Who?" technique, asking participants to nominate one another for roles they played during the experiencing stage.

- Interviewing pairs: asking one another "what" and "how" questions about the activity.

Publishing can be carried out through free discussion, but this requires that the facilitator be absolutely clear about the differences in the steps of the learning cycle and distinguish sharply among interventions in the discussion. Group members' energy is often focused on staying inside the activity, and they need to be nudged into separating themselves from it in order to learn. Structured techniques such as the preceding ones listed make the transition from stage one to stage two cleaner and easier. That, after all, is the job of the facilitator—to create clarity with ease.

Processing

This stage can be thought of as the fulcrum, or the pivotal step in experiential learning. It is the systematic examination of commonly shared experience by those persons involved. This is the "group dynamics" phase of the cycle, in which participants essentially reconstruct the patterns and interactions of the activity from the published individual reports. This "talking-through" part of the cycle is critical, and it cannot be either ignored or designed spontaneously if useful learning is to be developed. The facilitator needs to plan carefully how the processing will be carried out and focused toward the next stage, generalizing. Unprocessed data can be experienced as "unfinished business" by participants and can distract them from further learning. Selected techniques that can be used in the processing stage are listed below:

- Process observers: reports, panel discussions (observers are often unduly negative and need training in performing their functions).

- Thematic discussion: looking for recurring topics from the reports of individuals.

- Sentence completion: writing individual responses to such items as "The leadership was...," "Participation in this activity led to...."

- Questionnaires: writing individual responses to items developed for the particular activity.

- Data analysis: studying trends and correlations in ratings and adjectives elicited during the publishing stage.

- Key terms: posting a list of dimensions to guide the discussion.

- Interpersonal feedback: focusing attention on the effect of the role behaviors of significant members in the activity.

This step should be thoroughly worked through before going on to the next. Participants should be led to look at what happened in terms of dynamics but not in terms of "meaning." What occurred was real, of course, but it also was somewhat artificially contrived by the structure of the activity. It is important to keep in mind that a consciousness of the dynamics of the activity is critical for learning about human relations outside of the laboratory setting. Participants often anticipate the next step of the learning cycle and make premature generalization statements. The facilitator needs to make certain that the processing has been adequate before moving on.

Generalizing

An inferential leap has to be made at this point in the activity, from the reality inside the activity to the reality of everyday life outside the training session. The key question here is "So what?" Participants are led to focus their awareness on situations in their personal or work lives that are similar to those in the activity that they experienced. Their task is to abstract some principles that could be applied "outside." This step is what makes experiential learning activities practical; if it is omitted or glossed over, the learning is likely to be superficial. Here are some strategies for developing generalizations from the processing stage:

- Guided Imagery: guiding participants to imagine realistic situations "back home" and determining what they have learned in the discussion that might be applicable there.

- Truth with a little "t": writing statements from the processing discussion about what is "true" about the "real world."

- Individual analysis: writing "What I learned," "What I'm beginning to learn," "What I relearned."

- Key terms: posting topics such as "leadership," "communication," "feelings," etc., for potential generalizations.

- Sentence completion: writing completions to items such as "The effectiveness of shared leadership depends on...."

It is useful in this stage for the group interaction to result in a series of products—generalizations that are presented not only orally but also visually. This strategy helps to facilitate vicarious learning among participants. The facilitator needs to remain nonevaluative about what is learned, drawing out the reactions of others to generalizations that appear incomplete, undivided, or controversial. Participants sometimes anticipate the final stage of the learning cycle also, and they need to be kept on the track of clarifying what was learned before discussing what changes are needed.

In the generalizing stage it is possible for the facilitator to bring in theoretical and research findings to augment the learning. This practice provides a framework for the learning that has been produced inductively and checks the reality orientation of the process. But the practice may encourage dependence on the facilitator as the source of defensible knowledge and may lessen commitment to the final stage of the cycle. The outside information is not "owned" by the participants—a common phenomenon of *deductive* processes.

Applying

The final stage of the experiential learning cycle is the purpose for which the whole experiential learning activity is designed. The central question here is "Now what?" The facilitator helps participants apply generalizations to actual situations in which they are involved. Ignoring such discussion jeopardizes the probability that the learning will be useful. It is critical that attention be given to designing ways for individuals and/or groups to use the learning generated during the structured experience to plan more effective behavior. Several practices can be incorporated into this stage:

- Consulting pairs or trios: taking turns helping one another with back-home problem situations and applying generalizations.

- Goal setting: writing applications according to such goal criteria as specificity, performance, involvement, realism, and observability.

- Contracting: making explicit promises to one another about applications.

- Subgrouping: in interest groups, discussing specific generalizations in terms of what can be done more effectively.

- Practice session: role playing back-home situations to attempt changed behavior.

Individuals are more likely to implement their planned applications if they share them with others. Volunteers can be asked to report what they intend to do with what they have learned, and this can encourage others to experiment with their behavior also.

It is important to note that on the diagram of the experiential learning cycle there is a dotted arrow from "applying" to "experiencing." This is meant to indicate that the actual application of the learning is a new experience for the participant, to be examined inductively also. What structured experiences "teach" is a way of using one's everyday experiences as data for learning about human interactions, or "relearning how to learn." Actually, there are other ways to learn. For example, skills are best learned through practice toward an ideal model, knowledge of results, and positive reinforcement. Also, experiential learning activities do not readily facilitate the development of large-scale perspective; lecture-discussion methods are probably superior for such a purpose. What experiential learning does accomplish, though, is a sense of ownership over what is learned. This is most easily achieved by making certain that each stage of the learning cycle is developed adequately.

A GLOSSARY OF TERMS IN EXPERIENTIAL TRAINING

Trainers and group facilitators are notorious for their use of jargon. Those who use an "applied-behavioral-science" approach often use technical terms interchangeably, adding to the confusion of participants. The following listing is intended to help clarify this situation.

Activity	A design that creates a common experience to be studied and discussed by participants.
Case Study	Group discussion and problem solving from material about an actual situation.
Critique	Group evaluation of the effective and ineffective aspects of a learning design.
Deductive	A learning method that begins with "truth" and proceeds to its logical conclusions.
Deroling	Helping participants in a role play to extricate themselves from their assigned roles and to resume their normal interactions.
Didactic	Adjective describing a teaching approach in which information is imparted from an expert.
Energizer	Activity designed to develop readiness for participation in learning events; usually involves physical movement and fun.
Exercise	Repetitive activity, usually designed as a part of training to develop skills.
Experiencing	Phase I of the Experiential Learning Cycle; a learning activity to be discussed by participants afterwards.
Experiential	Adjective describing an approach to learning in which participants in an activity learn through reflection on the activity itself.

Experiential Learning Activity	A design for inductive learning through the implementation of the Experiential Learning Cycle; focuses on particular learning goals (also referred to as a Structured Experience).
Experiential Learning Cycle	A model of an inductive learning process consisting of five phases: Experiencing, Publishing, Processing, Generalizing, and Applying.
Experiment	A (structured) activity with outcomes that are unpredictable.
Facilitator	A person who uses experiential methods to promote learning; literally, "one who makes things easy."
Feedback	Information about the effects of one's behavior.
Game	An activity that is engaged in for its own sake; usually connotes fun and competition or chance.
Icebreaker	An activity to help participants to release anxiety at the beginning of a training event; usually fun, involving becoming acquainted with one another.
Inductive	A learning method that is based on the discovery of "truth" from the examination of experience.
Input	Exposition of information or theory; contribution to a discussion.
Instrument	Paper-and-pencil device used to inventory or rate oneself or a system.
Intensive Growth Group	Unstructured experience focused on the here-and-now; may be T-group, encounter, therapy, counseling, or marathon.
Item	A component of an instrument.

Likert Scale	Type of attitude-measurement scale developed by Rensis Likert; usually "strongly agree, agree, undecided, disagree, strongly disagree."
Model	(1) Theoretical explanation of a complex set of phenomena; (2) ideal behavior type.
Modeling	(1) Demonstrating effective behavior; (2) developing a theoretical explanation of a process.
Norms	(1) Expected behaviors; (2) statistical summary of responses to an instrument.
Package	A self-contained training design that is completely developed, with little or no flexibility.
Parameter	Characteristic factor, goal, or limitation; what the facilitator has to work with in creating a learning design.
Participation Training	Group discussion that includes learning how to be a more effective group member.
Processing	Group discussion of the results of a learning activity; Phase III of the Experiential Learning Cycle.
Publishing	Sharing reactions and observations; talking about one's experience during a learning activity; Phase II of the Experiential Learning Cycle.
Questionnaire	An instrument that does not have correct answers; used in surveys.
Reinforcement	Anything that raises the probability that a response will be repeated.
Response Format	A scale or method used by participants in reacting to the item of an instrument.

Role Playing	A design for learning in which participants act out a situation through assigned parts that they play spontaneously.
Self-Assessment	Looking inward, usually through a learning activity.
Self-Disclosure	Communicating about oneself to others; letting others know about one's private self.
Set	Psychological condition prior to an activity; attitudinal predisposition; expectations.
Simulation	Interactive learning package designed to re-create or mirror a larger, more complex situation in order to sponsor learning.
Skill Building	Developing effective behavior through practice toward an ideal type, with both knowledge of results (feedback) and reinforcement.
Structured Experience	A design for inductive learning through the implementation of the Experiential Learning Cycle; focuses on particular learning goals (also referred to as an Experiential Learning Activity).
Test	An instrument with "correct" answers.
Win-Lose	Adjective describing a competitive situation in which there must be a loser in order for there to be a winner.

Although these terms are not technically precise, we have found it useful to insist on making sharp distinctions between them for the sake of clarity and ease of comprehension. Undoubtedly many persons would argue for even more specific and exclusive definitions.

INTRODUCTION TO EXPERIENTIAL LEARNING ACTIVITIES

Experiential learning activities—designed to focus on individual behavior, constructive feedback, processing, and psychological integration—are infinitely varied and variable. They can be adapted easily to the particular needs of the group, the aim of a training design, or the special competencies of the training facilitator. In publishing experiential learning activities, we assume that facilitators are, by their nature, innovators. As one friend remarked, "I use your materials all the time, but I almost never do things the way you guys describe them."

We are concerned that all human-interaction training experiences have adequate processing so that the participants are able to integrate their learning without the stress generated by unresolved feelings or a lack of understanding. It is here that the expertise of the facilitator becomes crucial. If the activity is to be responsive to the needs of the participants, the facilitator must be able to assist the participants in successfully processing the data that emerge from that experience. Thus, an activity should be selected on the basis of two criteria—the facilitator's competence and the participants' needs.

CONSIDERATIONS IN DEVELOPING AN EXPERIENTIAL LEARNING ACTIVITY

To further the creation and availability of these valuable materials, we are including some points and questions to be considered when developing an experiential learning activity.

Goals. These should be limited in number and stated in language that participants can understand. A good goal is specific in that it states exactly what will occur; it is less specific in terms of the result of that occurrence, in order to permit inductive learning, i.e., learning through discovery. For example, a goal may be "to examine" or "to explore" the effects of collaboration and competition. The activity will involve those two dynamics. What is learned, however, may differ from participant to participant, depending on the participants' backgrounds and their unique experiences during the activity. A goal is performance oriented, to guide the person toward what he or she is going to do; it involves the individual in the goal objective; it is observable, so that other people can see the result; and, most important, it is realistic. For maximum effectiveness, a goal must be attainable.

Group Size. The minimum and maximum number of participants, the optimum size of the group, and the number and size of subgroups should be noted where relevant. If there are extra participants, how should they be utilized? (They could, for example, be designated as observers or added to subgroups.)

Time Required. This should be a realistic expectation, based on actual trials of the experience. Adequate time must be allowed for sharing and processing the learnings. If the activity requires a long period of time, can it be divided into more than one session?

Materials. The criteria here are easy availability, utility, and uncomplicated preparation. The specific forms, sheets of information, or work sheets needed and the quantities of each should be listed. If appropriate, an observer sheet should be devised for the activity. Audiovisual aids (such as felt-tipped pens, newsprint, sound or film equipment), pencils and paper, and any other special materials should be indicated if applicable.

Physical Setting. What are the participants' needs: Must groups be private, quiet, isolated? Do participants sit around tables or on the floor? Do they need writing surfaces? Can the experience take place outdoors? Do rooms need to be specially designated or arranged for certain groups or subgroups? Easily movable furniture is usually desirable to aid in the flexibility of the group.

Process. This is a step-by-step procedure that should indicate what the facilitator does and says and what the participants do in the appropriate sequence. The beginning and end of each step should be specified. A time estimate may be useful for each step or phase.

Variations. Adaptations may be noted to vary the activity's content, sequence, use of observers, time for each step, materials, size of groups, complexity of process, and use with intact groups.

Credit Line. Ideas and designs of others should be acknowledged; if more than one author is to be credited, the authors' names should appear in the order of the significance of their contributions, with the senior author or contributor listed first.

Work Sheets. These should be designed and written so that they contain sufficient room in which the participants may write, are simple and easy to reproduce, have clear instructions, and are necessary and meaningful to the activity. Whenever possible, each work sheet should be on one page, with type large enough to read easily. It is practical to have the work sheet contain its own instructions. If it does not, it should tell the participant that the facilitator will give oral instructions. Sources for work sheets should be acknowledged.

Handouts. This format is especially useful for a discussion of the theory underlying new behavior suggested by the activity. Unless necessary, participants should not be allowed to read handout materials while the process is running. However, if handouts are to be provided, the participants should be told at the beginning of the experience so that they will not prepare to take notes.

CONSIDERATIONS IN USING EXPERIENTIAL LEARNING ACTIVITIES

Certain questions need to be asked by the facilitator who is considering using an experiential learning activity as an intervention in a training event. This set of considerations constitutes a self-examination that is intended to help the facilitator select and develop designs that are both relevant and effective.

What are the goals of this group and why was it formed? Experiential learning activities are designed for a variety of purposes, but their most effective use is within programs that are aimed at specific learning goals. The facilitator needs to keep these goals in mind at all times.

At what stage is the group in its development or what stage is it likely to reach? Different issues surface at various stages of group development, and some activities are particularly useful at some points in group life. A feedback design may be inappropriate in the earliest stages but highly beneficial after the group has a brief history.

What is my contract with the group? Some groups expect the facilitator to "run" everything. It is important to minimize the gap in expectations between the facilitator and the participants. Using too many experiential learning activities may reinforce dependency on the part of the members, and they may turn to the facilitator to introduce an activity rather than confronting their own behavior. The facilitator needs to make it clear that each member is responsible for his or her own learning.

Why is it important that I intervene? Because it is possible for facilitators to meet their own needs at the participants' expense, it is important that facilitators assess their own motives for intervening into the interaction among members. Useful distinctions can be made between making things happen, letting things happen, and being a part of what is happening. One useful thought is "When in doubt, wait."

Why does this particular intervention appeal to me? It may be that the activity seems appropriate because it would be "fun" to do. However, the overriding consideration should be the learning needs of the participants at a particular point in the group's development. One should be careful not to overuse any given activity; this might indicate that the facilitator has "a solution in search of a problem."

How ready are these participants to take risks or to experiment? Some activities, such as guided imagery and nonverbal activities, are threatening to many participants and may evoke anxiety and defensiveness rather than openness to learning. It is useful, however, to establish an experimentation norm in laboratory education, and participants should be expected to "stretch" somewhat.

What content modifications can I make for an effective, appealing design? Local issues and concerns can be incorporated into materials and processes in order to heighten the possibility of the transfer of training. Such advance preparation can have a high payoff in developing work norms and avoiding "game playing." Roles, goals, company policies, issues, cases, etc., can be gathered with the help of participants.

What advance preparations need to be made? Appropriate rooms, with the right kinds of furniture and equipment, should be scheduled. The staff may need to be prepared. Materials must be duplicated and assembled. Sometimes it is helpful to prearrange the furniture so that participants are seated in preparation for the first phase of the process.

How rigid are the time restraints for the session? It is necessary not to generate more data than can be adequately processed within the session. It is better not to use an activity than to leave too much data "hanging" at the end. One consideration is to anticipate which elements of the design can be speeded up or expanded, if necessary.

How am I going to set up the processing? Because the processing of the data generated by the activity is more important than the activity itself, this planning phase should be carefully considered. A number of strategies can be used, such as process observers who have been briefed and who are using comprehensive guides; lecturettes; instrumented processing with brief questionnaires; subgrouping; empty chair or group-on-group techniques; and interviewing. Some of the data may be saved for use in later training designs.

How will I evaluate the effectiveness of the design? Because experiential learning activities are best employed in an atmosphere directed toward specific goals, some assessment of the extent to which the goals of a given activity were met is necessary. Such a study may be impressionistic and/or "objective," but it needs to be planned beforehand. The facilitator needs to decide the basis for judging whether or not or to what degree the aims of a particular intervention were accomplished.

FAILURE OF EXPERIENTIAL LEARNING ACTIVITIES

Experiential learning activities can "fail." That is, they may not produce the predicted results, or they may produce unexpected results.

Usually, such failure occurs when the experiential model is truncated or abbreviated or when it is inadequately implemented. Each step in the model is an essential part of the entire sequence; each needs sufficient attention to effect its full impact. Inadequate processing is the most common cause of the failure of the model.

Unfortunately, failure on the part of any facilitator only increases the chances that other facilitators may encounter difficulty in their attempts to present an experiential learning activity. If participants in a learning activity have previously had ineffective training experiences, it is likely that they will be more resistant to, and less inclined to involve themselves in, future training experiences.

Thus, the question of the "failure" of experiential learning activities becomes significant. Failure promotes subsequent failure. For this reason, we are stressing here the need for facilitators to confront the demands and requirements of the experiential model so that they—and their colleagues who follow them—may gather the rewards and benefits the model offers.

The implications of the model stress the necessity for adequate planning and sufficient time for each step. An appropriate structure is especially important for processing, generalizing, and applying. When handled with care, concern, and skill, the experiential approach is invaluable for group facilitators in the fields of applied behavioral science and organizational training and development.

NUMBERING OF EXPERIENTIAL LEARNING ACTIVITIES

Experiential learning activities are numbered consecutively throughout the series of *Handbooks* and *Annuals,* in the order of the publication of the volumes.

Experiential Learning Activity	Publication
1 through 24	Volume I, *Handbook*
25 through 48	Volume II, *Handbook*
49 through 74	Volume III, *Handbook*
75 through 86	1972 *Annual*
87 through 100	1973 *Annual*
101 through 124	Volume IV, *Handbook*
125 through 136	1974 *Annual*
137 through 148	1975 *Annual*
149 through 172	Volume V, *Handbook*
173 through 184	1976 *Annual*
185 through 196	1977 *Annual*
197 through 220	Volume VI, *Handbook*
221 through 232	1978 *Annual*
233 through 244	1979 *Annual*
245 through 268	Volume VII, *Handbook*
269 through 280	1980 *Annual*
281 through 292	1981 *Annual*
293 through 316	Volume VIII, *Handbook*
317 through 328	1982 *Annual*
329 through 340	1983 *Annual*
341 through 364	Volume IX, *Handbook*
365 through 376	1984 *Annual*
377 through 388	1985 *Annual*
389 through 412	Volume X, *Handbook*
413 through 424	1986 *Annual*
425 through 436	1987 *Annual*
437 through 448	1988 *Annual*
449 through 460	1989 *Annual*
461 through 472	1990 *Annual*
473 through 484	1991 *Annual*
485 through 496	1992 *Annual*
497 through 508	1993 *Annual*
509 through 520	1994 *Annual*

CLASSIFICATION OF EXPERIENTIAL LEARNING ACTIVITIES

Professionals who use the experiential learning activities in the *Handbooks* and *Annuals* need an easy and reliable way to choose activities that would be appropriate for particular training events. To meet this need, we have categorized the 520 activities in this *Reference Guide*—all of the activities previously published in the ten volumes of the *Handbook* and the twenty-three volumes of the *Annual*—into the following six major categories, based on the *goals* of the activity:

- Individual Development: activities that focus on the expansion of personal insight and awareness.

- Communication: activities that emphasize verbal, nonverbal, and metaverbal communication patterns and enhance skills in these areas in both interpersonal and group situations.

- Problem Solving: activities that focus on the skills that constitute effective problem solving.

- Groups: activities that focus on how individuals affect group functioning and how groups organize and function to accomplish objectives.

- Teams: activities that focus on how work teams organize and function to accomplish objectives.

- Consulting and Facilitating: activities that help to develop the skills of internal and external consultants and facilitators, in both organizational and group settings.

- Leadership: activities that emphasize the skills needed for effective leadership behavior.

Each major category has been divided into subcategories in order to help the trainer to select activities more accurately. The same subcategories may be included under more than one major category; for example, "How Groups Work" appears under both "Groups" and "Teams." Of course, experiential learning activities may be used for any number of goals other than those indicated; however, the trainer who uses this categorization will be more likely to find activities that have been designed to meet his or her particular goals. It is true that a sophisticated classification system necessarily involves fine distinctions about the placement of a particular activity. The primary intent of this system is to help the user to find materials quickly and with discrimination. We support and encourage facilitators to develop their own cross-referencing system for using activities.

Definitions of the subcategory topics within major categories follow.

Individual Development

Sensory Awareness: activities that focus on personal awareness and skills through the exploration of the senses.

Self-Disclosure: activities that teach the ability to reveal oneself to others.

Sex Roles: activities that help a person to see assumptions he or she may have about sex roles and the effects of these assumptions.

Diversity: activities that expand awareness of personal stereotypes and prejudices and their effects.

Life/Career Planning: activities that allow a person to evaluate the present and the future of his or her career or life.

Communication

Awareness: activities that illustrate what happens when people communicate, either verbally or nonverbally.

Building Trust: activities to create trust and a climate of openness and learning.

Conflict: activities that develop skills to recognize and deal with interpersonal-conflict situations.

Feedback: activities that promote awareness of how others can help a person to understand the impact of his or her behavior and that encourage acceptance of the opinions or feelings of others.

Listening: skill-building activities that help people to listen actively.

Styles: activities that identify communication styles and deal with issues of style in interpersonal interactions.

Problem Solving

Generating Alternatives: activities that offer practice in this early step in problem solving.

Information Sharing: activities that demonstrate the importance of sharing information effectively in problem solving.

Consensus/Synergy: activities to develop the group's skills at reaching general agreement and commitment to its decisions and goals.

Action Planning: activities that teach the skill of action planning.

Groups

How Groups Work: activities that help to develop skills in observing what is taking place within a group.

Competition/Collaboration: activities that deal with both the competitive tendencies that emerge within groups and the appropriateness of collaborative behavior.

Conflict: activities that develop skills to surface and handle conflicts in a group.

Negotiating/Bargaining: activities that deal with the effects of win-win and win-lose approaches to resolving differences.

Teams

How Groups Work: activities that help team members to develop skills in observing what is taking place within their work team.

Roles: activities that identify and explore various roles played by members of a work team.

Problem Solving/Decision Making: activities that teach these necessary skills within a work team.

Feedback: activities that encourage the exchange of effective feedback within a work team.

Conflict and Intergroup Issues: activities that develop skills to surface and handle conflicts within a work team and between work groups.

Consulting and Facilitating

Consulting: Awareness: activities that help people to be aware of the forces that affect the functioning of their organizations.

Consulting: Diagnosing/Skills: activities that focus on diagnosing organizational problems that develop the skills of the internal or external consultant.

Facilitating: Opening: activities designed to "warm up" members of a learning group that is meeting for the first time; to recharge the group when energy is low; or to create a climate of trust, openness, and learning within the group.

Facilitating: Blocks to Learning: activities developed to deal with situations in which learning is blocked through the interference of other dynamics—conscious or unconscious—in the group.

Facilitating: Skills: activities designed to develop the facilitative abilities of trainers, group leaders, and group facilitators.

Facilitating: Closing: activities to use at the end of a training event.

Leadership

Ethics: activities that allow individuals to examine the ethical implications of their assumptions and behaviors.

Interviewing/Appraisal: activities to develop skills needed in interviewing and appraisal situations.

Motivation: activities that deal with issues of motivation in interactions between leaders and members of a group.

Diversity/Stereotyping: activities that look at values and prejudices within personal and organizational contexts and how these factors affect the functioning of a group or organization.

Styles: activities that identify leadership styles and deal with issues of style in interactions between leaders and members of a group.

Classifying these materials is somewhat arbitrary, because they can be adapted for a variety of training purposes. Although any given activity could belong to a number of classifications, we have listed each only once, categorizing it in the area of its most probable use.

INDIVIDUAL DEVELOPMENT: Sensory Awareness

(III-31)   **056. Feelings and Defenses:** A Spontaneous Lecture (Time required: about thirty minutes.)

- To study feelings significant to group members and defenses they use.

- To help group members take responsibility for their own learning.

(III-94)   **071. Lemons:** A Sensory-Awareness Activity (Time required: one hour.)

- To increase sensory awareness.

('72-59)   **085. Growth and Name Fantasy,** by Tony Banet (Time required: approximately forty-five minutes.)

- To provide group participants with an opportunity to review, in fantasy, the phases of growth and development they have accomplished.

- To review their sense of individual identity.

(IV-92)   **119. Group Exploration:** A Guided Fantasy, by Leo Berman (Time required: approximately one hour.)

- To allow individuals to share their means of coping with fear and stress as well as their personal responses to pleasure.

('74-84)   **136. Relaxation and Perceptual Awareness:** A Workshop, by John L. Hipple, Michael Hutchins, and James Barott (Time required: three hours.)

- To learn basic techniques of physical relaxation, breathing processes, and self-awareness.

- To experience one's physical state of existence and personal perceptions of inner and outer reality and fantasy.

(VI-10)   **199. T'ai Chi Chuan:** An Introduction to Movement Awareness, by David X. Swenson (Time required: approximately one hour.)

- To increase body self-awareness.

- To develop integrated, relaxed, economical, and balanced movement and activity.

- To facilitate a feeling of "centeredness" in the here-and-now.

(VI-102)   **214. Roles Impact Feelings:** A Role Play, by Maury Smith (Time required: approximately two and one-half hours.)

- To enable participants to become aware of some of the roles they play.

- To discover how roles produce feelings.

(VIII-30)   **300. Projections:** Interpersonal Awareness Expansion, by Bernard Nisenholz (Time required: one and one-half hours.)

- To help participants to explore the process of projection.

- To provide an opportunity for participants to recognize how and what they project about others.

- To enable participants to become more aware of the part they play in the outcome of unpleasant situations.

INDIVIDUAL DEVELOPMENT: Self-Disclosure

(I-65)   **013. Johari Window:** An Experience in Self-Disclosure and Feedback (Time required: approximately two hours.)

- To introduce the concept of the Johari Window.

- To permit participants to process data about themselves in terms of self-disclosure and feedback.

(I-88)   **020. Graphics:** Self-Disclosure Activities (Time required: varies.)

- To generate self-disclosure data through graphics.

(III-109)   **074. Personal Journal:** A Self-Evaluation (Time required: any number of periods of ten to fifteen minutes each, depending on the design of the laboratory or workshop.)

- To heighten participants' awareness of the sequence of events and the corresponding emotional development which takes place in a laboratory or workshop.

- To aid in self-disclosure.

- To provide a post-laboratory or post-workshop resource for reinforcing learning.

('73-13)   **090. Make Your Own Bag:** Symbolic Self-Disclosure, by Kris Lawson (Time required: approximately one hour and forty-five minutes.)

- To raise levels of trust and openness in a group.

- To make group members aware of themselves and others as persons.

(IV-30)   **109. Growth Cards:** Experimenting with New Behavior, by Meyer Cahn (Time required: approximately two hours.)

- To develop an accepting atmosphere for risk taking and self-disclosure.

- To give those within a larger laboratory community a legitimate entry point for the provision of individual feedback to participants in other groups.

- To supply participants with specific, individual feedback to aid them in making decisions concerning an agenda for modifying their own behavior.

- To increase understanding and acceptance of personality components which decrease interpersonal effectiveness.

- To strengthen individual commitment to behavioral change through open verbalization and the development of a method or prescription for modification.

- To reinforce group skills of decision making and task performance.

(IV-104)   **122. Expressing Anger:** A Self-Disclosure Exercise, by Gary R. Gemmill (Time required: approximately forty-five minutes.)

- To study styles of expressing anger in a group setting.

- To study effects of anger in a group setting.

- To legitimize the presence and expression of anger within groups.

- To identify behaviors that elicit anger in others.

- To explore ways of coping with anger.

(IV-107)   **123. Stretching:** Identifying and Taking Risks, by Robert R. Kurtz (Time required: approximately two hours.)

- To help participants become aware of interpersonal behavior that is risky for them.

- To increase participants' awareness of the relationship between risk-taking behavior and the attainment of personal growth goals.

- To encourage risk-taking behavior as a way of expanding participants' behavioral repertoire.

('74-20)   **129. Forced-Choice Identity:** A Self-Disclosure Activity, by John J. Sherwood (Time required: approximately two hours.)

- To gain insight about oneself.

- To facilitate self-disclosure and feedback.

- To encourage community building.

- To enhance enjoyment of the group experience through a change-of-pace activity.

('76-49)   **181. Boasting:** A Self-Enhancement Activity, by Jack J. Rosenblum and John E. Jones (Time required: approximately one hour and fifteen minutes.)

- To help participants identify, own, and share their personal strengths.

- To explore feelings and reactions to sharing "boasts" with other participants.

- To experience the enhanced sense of personal power in announcing one's strengths to others.

('76-51) **182. The Other You:** Awareness Expansion, by Anthony J. Reilly (Time required: approximately two and one-half hours.)

- To increase personal self-awareness.

- To provide participants an opportunity to experiment with new behavior.

- To help participants integrate new data into their self-concepts.

(VIII-61) **306. Praise:** Giving and Receiving Positive Feedback, by Thomas J. Mason (Time required: one and one-half to two hours.)

- To develop an awareness of one's own accomplishments.

- To practice giving public recognition to others.

- To become aware of one's responses to recognition from others.

('82-29) **321. Introjection:** Identifying Significant Beliefs, by Bernard Nisenholz (Time required: one to one and one-half hours.)

- To help participants to recognize the sources of their significant beliefs.

- To provide an opportunity for participants to identify their current personal reactions to their significant beliefs.

- To enable participants to reconsider which significant beliefs they would like to retain and which they would like to modify.

(IX-58)   **349. Personality Traits:** Self-Discovery and Disclosure, by William J. Schiller (Time required: approximately one hour.)

- To assist the participants in gaining insight about themselves.

- To facilitate self-disclosure.

('88-21)   **438. Understanding the Need for Approval:** Toward Personal Autonomy, by Allen Johnson (Time required: one and one-half to two hours.)

- To help participants understand how the need for approval affects behavior.

- To help participants become aware of how they are externally directed.

- To introduce techniques for fostering self-actualization.

- To encourage participants to contract for internal control.

('88-89)   **448. The Golden Egg Award:** Facilitating Openness, by C. Philip Alexander (Time required: approximately one hour and ten minutes.)

- To assist the participants in building a group norm of openness.

- To promote self-disclosure and to develop the participants' ability to interact openly during group work.

- To enhance the participants' understanding of "mistakes" as opportunities for learning.

INDIVIDUAL DEVELOPMENT: Sex Roles

(III-57)   **062. Polarization:** A Demonstration, by John E. Jones and Johanna J. Jones (Time required: approximately two hours.)

- To explore the experience of interpersonal polarization—its forms and effects.

- To study conflict management and resolution.

('73-26)   **095. Sex-Role Stereotyping,** by Mary Carson (Time required: approximately two hours.)

- To make distinctions between thoughts and feelings about sex-role stereotyping.

- To examine one's own reactions to sexism in a mixed group.

- To link feeling feedback to observable behavior.

- To avoid over-generalization.

- To explore the experience of interpersonal polarization—its forms and effects.

- To study conflict resolution.

('76-63)   **184. Sex-Role Attributes:** A Collection of Activities (Time required: varies with each activity.)

- To expand personal awareness.

- To explore the cultural biases and prejudices that the sexes have regarding each other.

(VI-106)   **215. Who Gets Hired?:** A Male/Female Role Play, by L.V.
Entrekin and G.N. Soutar (Time required: one to one
and one-half hours.)

- To clarify one's personal values regarding sex
  discrimination.

- To examine the values held in common on this subject
  within a group.

- To explore whether groups of different sexual
  composition have differences in such values.

- To study the way in which such issues are resolved
  within a group.

- To gain insight into the subtle aspects of
  discrimination.

('78-36)   **226. Sexual Assessment:** Self-Disclosure, by Paul S.
Weikert (Time required: approximately two and one-half
hours.)

- To share sexual perceptions, feelings, attitudes, values,
  behaviors, and expectations.

- To clarify one's sexuality through self-insight.

- To gain insight into the sexual dimensions of other
  persons.

(VII-19)   **248. Alpha II:** Clarifying Sexual Values, by Don Keyworth
(Time required: two to two and one-half hours.)

- To explore attitudes regarding sexual mores.

- To compare sexual values with others.

- To practice group consensus seeking.

(VII-24) **249. Sexual Values:** Relationship Clarification, by Paul S. Weikert (Time required: one and one-half hours.)

- To identify one's own values about a sexual relationship.

- To become aware of the sexual values of others.

- To increase awareness of the many components of sexual relationships.

(VII-85) **258. Sex-Role Attitudes:** Personal Feedback, by Brian P. Holleran (Time required: approximately two to three hours.)

- To develop and understanding of the way in which sex-based attitudes influence and are inferred from communication.

- To discuss attitudes and prejudices about sexes in a nonthreatening environment.

- To increase awareness of and provide feedback on one's own attitudes, beliefs, and behaviors in regard to sex differences.

(VII-146) **268. Sexual Values in Organizations:** An OD Role Play, by Peggy Morrison (Time required: three hours.)

- To identify a range of personal, ethical, professional, and organizational considerations related to sexual relationships that occur between members of an organization.

- To determine the effect of such relationships on individual as well as organizational effectiveness.

('80-26)   **272. Sexual Attraction:** A Written Role Play, by Jeanne
Bosson Driscoll and Rosemary A. Bova (Time required:
approximately one hour and forty-five minutes.)

- To explore the dynamics of sexual attraction among
coworkers.

- To heighten awareness of the effect that assumptions
can have on the shaping of an evolving relationship.

- To provide an opportunity for participants to explore
their personal interpretations of, assumptions about,
and responses to issues regarding sexual attraction.

(VIII-58)   **305. Sexism in Advertisements:** Exploring Stereotypes, by
Anne J. Burr, Deborah C.L. Griffith, David B. Lyon,
Gertrude E. Philpot, Gary N. Powell, and Dorianne L.
Sehring (Time required: approximately one and one-half
hours.)

- To become more aware of sex-role stereotyping in
advertisements.

- To identify elements of advertisements that do or do
not reflect sex-role stereotyping.

- To increase awareness of the effects of social
conditioning.

(IX-152)   **362. The Promotion:** Value Clarification, by Janet Lee
Mills (Time required: two hours and fifteen minutes.)

- To provide an opportunity for the participants to
practice identifying and clarifying values.

- To help the participants to become aware of some of
the factors that affect their own value judgments as
well as those of others.

('86-21)   **415. Raising Elizabeth:** Socializing Occupational Choices, by Janet Mills (Time required: approximately two hours.)

- To explore socialization factors that predispose (women's) occupational choices, aspirations, and successes.

- To put these socialization factors into a personal context.

('88-9)   **437. The Problem with Men/Women is...:** Sex-Role Assumptions, by J. Rose Farber (Time required: approximately two hours.)

- To help participants to identify their own and others' assumptions about role expectations for men and women.

- To explore attitudes and feelings that surface when the participants begin comparing their assumptions and role expectations.

- To allow the participants to experience arguing in favor of a point of view with which they personally disagree.

('89-17)   **450. The Girl and the Sailor:** Value Clarification (Time required: approximately two hours.)

- To help participants clarify values.

- To develop participants' awareness of factors affecting their own value judgments and those of others.

- To demonstrate how values affect relationships and group decisions.

('90-45)   **466. Tina Carlan:** Resolving Sexual Harassment in the Workplace, by John A. Sample (Time required: approximately three hours and fifteen minutes.)

- To develop the participants' awareness of legal issues in connection with sexual harassment complaints.

- To provide the participants with a systematic process for investigating and resolving sexual harassment within an organization.

- To provide the participants with a group learning forum for how to resolve sexual harassment in the workplace.

- To provide an opportunity to examine personal reactions to the issue of sexual harassment.

INDIVIDUAL DEVELOPMENT: Diversity

(II-85)   **041. Status-Interaction Study:** A Multiple-Role-Play, by J. William Pfeiffer (Time required: forty-five minutes.)

- To explore effects of status differences and deference on interaction among members.

(III-41)   **058. Peer Perceptions:** A Feedback Experience, by John E. Jones (Time required: two to three hours.)

- To let each group member know to what degree he or she is seen to be similar to each other member.

- To study feeling reactions to being considered "different."

- To help each member define the dimensions of human similarity and dissimilarity he or she believes are important.

(III-62)   **063. Discrimination:** Simulation Activities (Time required: varies with each activity.)

- To simulate the experience of discrimination.

- To study phenomena of stereotyping people.

('73-23)   **094. Traditional American Values:** Intergroup Confrontation (Time required: approximately one and one-half hours.)

- To clarify one's own value system.

- To explore values held in common within a group.

- To study differences existing between groups.

- To begin to remove stereotypes held by members of different groups.

(IV-45)   **113. Growth Group Values:** A Clarification Exercise, by Ord Elliott and Dave Zellinger (Time required: approximately one and one-half hours.)

- To clarify one's own value system.

- To explore values held in common within a group.

- To study differences existing between groups.

- To begin to remove stereotypes held by members of different groups.

(IV-112)   **124. The In-Group:** Dynamics of Exclusion, by Gale Goldberg (Time required: approximately one and one-half hours.)

- To allow participants to experience consciously excluding and being excluded.

- To confront feelings which exclusion generates.

- To examine processes by which social identity is conferred by the excluding group and accepted by the excluded member.

('74-13)   **127. Leadership Characteristics:** Examining Values in Personnel Selection, by Charles Kormanski (Time required: approximately two hours.)

- To compare the results of individual decision making and group decision making.

- To explore values underlying leadership characteristics.

- To examine effects of value judgments on personnel selection.

(V-139)   **172. Group Composition:** A Selection Activity, by Gerald M. Phillips and Anthony G. Banet, Jr. (Time required: approximately one and one-half hours.)

- To explore the process of selection of group members.

- To assist facilitators in identifying their biases about group composition.

- To study similarities and differences between personal growth and psychotherapy groups.

(VI-25)   **203. Headbands:** Group Role Expectations, by Evelyn Sieburg (Time required: approximately forty-five minutes.)

- To experience the pressures of role expectations.

- To demonstrate the effects of role expectations on individual behavior in a group.

- To explore the effects of role pressures on total group performance.

(VI-92) **213. Sherlock:** An Inference Activity, by Rick Roskin (Time required: approximately one and one-half hours.)

■ To increase awareness of how prejudices, assumptions, and self-concepts influence perceptions and decisions.

■ To explore the relationship between observation, knowledge, and inference.

■ To help participants become aware of their personal preconceptions and biases.

(VI-114) **217. Negotiating Differences:** Avoiding Polarization, by David X. Swenson (Time required: approximately one hour.)

■ To identify the dimensions along which people may differ.

■ To explore the potential for persons to complement as well as conflict with each other, as a result of such differences.

■ To negotiate a contract for coordinating different personal style or opinions.

('78-40) **227. Young/Old Woman:** A Perception Experiment, by William R. Mulford (Time required: fifty minutes.)

■ To focus on individual reactions to the same stimulus.

■ To examine the effects of the immediate environment on an individual's perception.

('78-51) **229. Pygmalion:** Clarifying Personal Biases, by Richard L. Bunning (Time required: approximately forty-five minutes.)

■ To discover how preconceived ideas may influence collective and/or individual actions.

- To allow participants to assess their current behavior in terms of previous "scripting" and social pressure.

('79-38)   **239. Race from Outer Space:** An Awareness Activity, by Dorothy Goler Cash (Time required: one and one-half to two hours.)

- To compare qualities and skills needed to lead a single racial group and those needed to lead a mixed racial group.

- To increase awareness of social values and how these may differ among people and groups.

(VII-15)   **247. Prejudice:** An Awareness-Expansion Activity, by Richard Raine (Time required: one to one and one-half hours.)

- To share feelings and ideas about prejudices in a nonthreatening manner.

- To explore the validity of common prejudices.

(VII-108)   **262. Physical Characteristics:** Dyadic Perception Checking, by Allen J. Schuh (Time required: forty-five minutes to one hour.)

- To examine one's reactions to the physical characteristics of others.

- To learn to observe others more accurately.

- To study the effects of generalizing and stereotyping.

(VII-141)   **267. Whom to Choose:** Values and Group Decision Making, by Charles L. Eveland and Dorothy M. Hai (Time required: forty-five minutes to one hour.)

- To examine and make choices concerning one's own values.

■ To assess the degree to which members of a group have common values and the impact of this on group decision making.

■ To observe problem-solving strategies in groups.

('81-57)   **292. Data Survey:** Exploring Stereotypes, by Thomas J. Mulhern and Maureen A. Parashkevov (Time required: approximately one and one-half hours.)

■ To discover how one makes judgments about others on the basis of age, race, sex, or ethnic stereotypes.

■ To provide an opportunity to examine personal reactions to the issue of prejudice.

(VIII-21)   **298. Lifeline:** A Value-Clarification Activity, by Spencer H. Wyant (Time required: one and one-half hours.)

■ To increase awareness of social influences on the formation of attitudes, beliefs, values, and perceptions.

■ To examine personal development and growth in the context of political history, social movements, and popular culture.

■ To share differing values and orientations.

('83-72)   **338. Four Cultures:** Exploring Behavioral Expectations, by Dwight L. Gradin (Time required: two and one-half hours.)

■ To explore the effects of cultural behaviors or traits on others.

■ To experience cross-cultural encounters.

■ To increase awareness of how cultural mannerisms and rituals are derived from cultural attitudes.

(IX-14)   **344. All Iowans Are Naive:** Breaking Cultural Stereotypes,
by Michael Maggio and Nancy Allen Good (Time
required: approximately one and one-half hours.)

  ▪ To increase the participants' awareness of the
    stereotypes that they hold.

  ▪ To provide the participants with an opportunity to
    share their feelings about being the objects of
    stereotyping.

  ▪ To allow the participants to observe how others feel
    when they are negatively stereotyped.

(IX-172)   **364. AIRSOPAC:** Choosing a CEO, by Thomas H. Patten,
Jr. (Time required: two to two and one-half hours.)

  ▪ To explore values in executive decision making.

  ▪ To allow the participants to study procedures used by
    groups to evaluate individual differences among highly
    qualified people.

  ▪ To examine the impact of individual values and
    attitudes on group decision making.

('87-21)   **427. Doctor, Lawyer, Indian Chief:** Occupational
Stereotypes, by Mary Kirkpatrick Craig (Time required:
approximately two hours; more than seven pairs will
require more time.)

  ▪ To increase awareness of occupational stereotypes and
    of how they impact interpersonal relationships.

  ▪ To allow participants to discuss their feelings about
    occupational stereotyping.

('90-17)   **462. Life Raft:** Experiencing Values (Time required: one and one-half to two hours.)

- To help participants examine values in a dramatic way.

- To help participants identify feelings that accompany values.

- To encourage participants to explore feelings of self-worth.

- To increase awareness of how values influence group decision making.

('92-69)   **492. Zenoland:** Managing Culture Clash, by Josephine Lobasz-Mavromatis (Time required: approximately two hours and forty-five minutes.)

- To encourage the participants to consider the impact of cultural diversity on interactions among people.

- To foster the participants' awareness of and sensitivity to cultural attitudes and behaviors that are different from their own.

- To provide an opportunity for the participants to practice communicating and problem solving in a culturally diverse setting.

('94-9)   **509. First Impressions:** Examining Assumptions, by Steven E. Aufrecht (Time required: one hour and ten minutes to one and one-half hours.)

- To develop the participants' awareness of the ways in which they judge people and the ways in which others might judge them.

- To help the participants to see how their judgments about people cause them to make discriminatory decisions.

- To offer the participants an opportunity to discuss the implications of their first impressions and the judgments they make.

('94-17)   **510. Parole Board:** Exploring Individual and Group Values, by Arlette C. Ballew; based on Charles A. Beitz, Jr. (Time required: one hour and forty-five minutes to two hours.)

- To provide participants with an opportunity to explore their values concerning characteristics of individuals.

- To explore how individual values affect individual and group decisions.

- To explore the impact of group values on decision making.

INDIVIDUAL DEVELOPMENT: Life/Career Planning

(II-101)   **046. Life Planning:** A Programmed Approach (Time required: six hours, split into three two-hour periods.)

- To apply concepts of planned change to an individual's personal, interpersonal, and career development.

('79-9)   **233. Banners:** A Value-Clarification Activity, by Morris A. Graham (Time required: two to three hours.)

- To increase self-understanding and self-awareness of values, goals, and individual potential.

- To provide a forum for the public expression of personal values, potentials, and goal-achievement standards.

- To examine how life values, potential, and goal achievement affect decisions concerning personal needs and aspirations.

(VII-105)   **261. Wants Bombardment:** A Psychosynthesis Activity, by John E. Jones (Time required: approximately one and one-half hours.)

- To increase awareness of competing wants in one's life situation.

- To attempt to prioritize and/or synthesize one's wants.

('83-27)   **332. Career Renewal:** A Self-Inventory, by Karen J. Troy (Time required: approximately one hour.)

- To introduce the concept of job renewal.

- To enable participants to evaluate their present jobs in light of their stated career goals.

('85-15)   **378. Life Assessment and Planning:** Choosing the Future, by Allen J. Schuh (Time required: approximately four hours.)

- To help each participant to review personal values and past experiences and to establish a plan for the future.

- To offer the participants an opportunity to experience peer feedback.

(X-31)   **393. Work-Needs Assessment:** Achievement, Affiliation, and Power, by Patrick Doyle (Time required: one and one-half hours.)

- To develop the participants' awareness of the individual needs that motivate people to behave in certain ways in the workplace.

- To assist each participant in determining the needs that motivate him or her in the workplace.

(X-41)   **394. The Ego-Radius Model:** Evaluating and Planning Life Situations (Time required: two hours.)

- To assist each participant in clarifying and evaluating his or her present life situation and in planning the life situation desired in the future.

- To allow the participants to share their life situations with one another and to experience peer feedback as a part of the life-planning process.

('86-15)   **414. Dropping Out:** Exploring Changes in Life Style, by Michael R. Lavery (Time required: two and one-half to three hours.)

- To explore attitudes about the phenomenon of "dropping out."

- To identify professional and personal constraints that could motivate a person to "drop out" in order to change his or her life style.

('86-27)   **416. Roles:** Understanding Sources of Stress, by Patrick Doyle (Time required: approximately two hours.)

- To enable participants to explore the diverse roles they are expected to fill.

- To help participants to understand the characteristics of these roles.

- To illustrate the potential for stress caused by the different expectations of diverse roles.

- To provide an opportunity for the participants to develop solutions to their own role conflicts.

('88-31)   **439. Creating Ideal Personal Futures:** Using the Self-Fulfilling Prophecy, by John D. Adams (Time required: approximately one hour and fifty minutes.)

- To help the participants to develop awareness of the ways in which their nonconscious thought processes influence the results they achieve in life.

- To provide the participants with a technique for transforming inhibiting ways of thinking and behaving into ways of thinking and behaving that support the achievement of desired results.

- To help each participant establish a sense of his or her purpose in life and to write a statement of this purpose.

('90-9)   **461. Pie in the Sky:** Exploring Life Values, by Jule A. Patten and Thomas H. Patten, Jr. (Time required: approximately two hours.)

- To offer the participants an opportunity to examine their life and career values and aspirations.

- To provide the participants with the opportunity to examine their values.

- To help the participants to explore the degree of consistency between their expressed values and their actions.

('90-21)   **463. What's in It for Me?:** Clarifying Work Values, by Kathleen Kreis (Time required: approximately one and one-half hours.)

- To help the participants to determine what needs they seek to fulfill through their work.

- To help the participants to determine what needs are presently fulfilled through their work and how.

- To provide the participants with the opportunity to discuss ways to improve the match between what they seek and what they get from their work.

('91-9)   **473. Affirmations:** Positive Self-Talk, by Marian K. Prokop (Time required: approximately one hour.)

- To understand the nature and purpose of affirmations.

- To offer members of an intact work group the opportunity to practice developing and using affirmations.

('92-15)   **486. Supporting Cast:** Examining Personal Support Networks, by Marian K. Prokop (Time required: approximately two hours.)

- To acquaint the participants with the characteristics of a supporting cast—the network of people who help others to achieve their personal and professional goals.

- To offer the participants an opportunity to explore the roles that others play in their lives.

- To provide an opportunity for the participants to identify roles in their personal support networks that need to be filled or enhanced and to develop action plans to fill those needs.

('93-13)   **498. Career Visioning:** Strategic Problem Solving, by Neil Johnson and Jason Ollander-Krane (Time required: approximately three hours.)

- To offer participants an opportunity to generate various career-development options for themselves, to select among these options, and to develop a plan to achieve them.

- To acquaint participants with techniques of "visioning" and gap analysis.

COMMUNICATION: Awareness

(I-13)   **004. One-Way, Two-Way:** A Communications Experiment, adapted from H.J. Leavitt (Time required: approximately forty-five minutes.)

- To conceptualize the superior functioning of two-way communication through participatory demonstration.

- To examine the application of communication in family, social, and occupational settings.

(III-70)   **065. Think-Feel:** A Verbal Progression, by John E. Jones (Time required: forty-five minutes.)

- To make distinctions between thoughts and feelings.

- To learn to link feeling feedback to observable behavior.

- To practice empathizing.

(IV-27)   **108. Ball Game:** Controlling and Influencing Communication, by Ronald D. Jorgenson (Time required: approximately thirty minutes.)

- To explore the dynamics of assuming leadership in a group.

- To increase awareness of the power held by the member of a group who is speaking at any given time.

- To diagnose communication patterns in a group.

('74-18)   **128. Re-Owning:** Increasing Behavioral Alternatives, by H.B. Karp (Time required: approximately one hour.)

- To assist participants in exploring aspects of themselves that they might not be presently aware of or may be underutilizing.

- To extend the range of behavioral alternatives open for effective communication.

(V-13)   **152. Helping Relationships:** Verbal and Nonverbal Communication, by Clarke G. Carney (Time required: approximately thirty minutes.)

- To demonstrate the effects of posturing and eye contact on helping relationships.

- To focus group members' attention on the impact of their nonverbal behaviors on other individuals.

- To teach basic nonverbal listening and attending skills.

(V-16)   **153. Babel:** Interpersonal Communication, by Philip M. Ericson (Time required: approximately two hours.)

- To examine language barriers that contribute to breakdowns in communication.

- To demonstrate the anxieties and frustrations that may be felt when communicating under difficult circumstances.

- To illustrate the impact of nonverbal communication when verbal communication is ineffective and/or restricted.

('76-13)   **175. Blindfolds:** A Dyadic Experience, by James I.
Costigan and Arthur L. Dirks (Time required:
approximately one hour.)

- To demonstrate and experience the need for visual
  cues in perception and communication.

- To demonstrate the need for visual cues in the
  definition of "personal space."

('77-28)   **190. Letter Exchange:** A Dyadic Focus on Feelings, by
Arthur G. Kirn (Time required: approximately one hour.)

- To provide a practical, low-threat, repeatable
  framework for sharing feelings as a step toward
  building a dyadic relationship.

- To promote self-disclosure and interpersonal risk
  taking.

(VI-21)   **202. Dominoes:** A Communication Experiment, by
Stephan H. Putnam (Time required: approximately one
and one-half hours.)

- To enhance awareness of factors that help or hinder
  effective interpersonal communication.

- To explore the effect on task-oriented behavior of
  shared versus unshared responsibility.

('79-46)   **241. Blivet:** A Communication Experience, by Ken Myers,
Rajesh Tandon, and Howard Bowens, Jr. (Time required:
approximately one and one-half hours.)

- To demonstrate and experience one-way and two-way
  verbal communication.

- To demonstrate and experience barriers and aids to
  verbal communication.

- To explore the effects of different status positions on interpersonal communication.

(VII-28)   **250. Meanings Are in People:** Perception Checking, by Jack N. Wismer (Time required: one to three hours.)

- To demonstrate that meanings are not in words but in the people who use them and hear them.

- To illustrate that our perceptions of words attribute positive, neutral, and negative meanings to them.

(VII-34)   **251. Mixed Messages:** A Communication Experiment, by Branton K. Holmberg and Daniel W. Mullene (Time required: approximately forty-five minutes to one hour.)

- To explore the dynamics of receiving verbal and nonverbal communication cues that are in conflict with one another.

- To examine how nonverbal cues can convey listener attitudes that can affect the communication process.

- To develop an understanding of the importance and impact of being direct and congruent in all forms of interpersonal communication.

('81-28)   **286. Gestures:** Perceptions and Responses, by Stella Lybrand Norman (Time required: approximately one and one-half hours.)

- To provide an opportunity for participants to examine the perceptual biases operating in their interpretations of gestures.

- To increase awareness of the ambiguity inherent in various forms of nonverbal communication.

■ To demonstrate how one gesture can elicit different feeling responses among different persons.

■ To examine the principle that verbal and nonverbal communication must be congruent to be effective.

(VIII-64)　**307. Maze:** One-Way and Two-Way Communication, by Gilles L. Talbot (Time required: approximately one and one-half to two hours.)

■ To experience the effects of free versus restricted communication in accomplishing a task.

■ To explore the impact of communication processes on the development of trust between a leader and a follower.

('83-14)　**330. Feelings:** Verbal and Nonverbal Congruence, by Stella Lybrand Norman (Time required: one to one and one-half hours.)

■ To provide an opportunity to compare verbal and nonverbal components of feelings.

■ To develop awareness of the congruence between verbal and nonverbal components of feelings.

■ To increase sensitivity to the feelings of others.

(IX-5)　**341. Synonyms:** Sharing Perceptions Between Groups, by Phil Leamon (Time required: approximately one hour.)

■ To offer two different groups an opportunity to compare the ways in which they perceive and talk about their worlds.

■ To illustrate that people's language both expands and limits their worlds.

■ To improve understanding between two groups.

(X-55)   **396. In Other Words:** Building Oral-Communication Skills (Time required: approximately one and one-half hours.)

■ To acquaint the participants with some useful tips regarding effective oral communication.

■ To allow the participants to practice translating long, written messages into short but accurate and effective oral ones.

■ To offer the participants an opportunity to give and receive feedback about the effectiveness of their translations and their delivery.

(X-62)   **397. Taking Responsibility:** Practice in Communicating Assumptions, by Gilles L. Talbot (Time required: two hours.)

■ To develop the participants' understanding of the effects of assumptions on oral communication.

■ To offer the participants an opportunity to practice devising comments that demonstrate their willingness to assume responsibility for stating their assumptions.

(X-68)   **398. Pass It On:** Simulating Organizational Communication, by Linda Costigan Lederman and Lea P. Stewart (Time required: one hour and forty-five minutes.)

■ To enhance the participants' understanding of the complexity of oral communication patterns within an organization.

■ To illustrate what happens to messages that are transmitted orally through several different channels within an organization.

- To explore ways to improve oral communication within an organization.

('86-35) **417. Shades of Difference:** Exploring Metaverbal Communication, by Arlette C. Ballew (Time required: approximately two and one-half hours.)

- To demonstrate the impact that metaverbal aspects of communication have on the perception and interpretation of meaning.

- To allow the participants to practice using metaverbal aspects of communication.

('88-39) **440. E-Prime:** Distinguishing Facts from Opinions, by Gilles L. Talbot (Time required: approximately one hour and five minutes.)

- To foster the participants' awareness of how they speak about others and how they interpret comments about others.

- To assist the participants in distinguishing definitive from associative attributes (facts from opinions) used in conversation.

('90-29) **464. Words Apart:** Bridging the Communication Gap, by Mark Maier (Time required: one hour.)

- To help the participants to become aware of gender influences on conversation style.

- To provide the participants with the opportunity to experience artificial restrictions on their conversational styles.

- To help the participants to become aware of conversational patterns and styles.

('91-15)   **474. Supportive Versus Defensive Climates:** How Would You Say...?, by J.C. Bruno Teboul (Time required: one hour and twenty minutes.)

- To acquaint participants with six supportive and six defensive communication dimensions.

- To develop participants' abilities to recognize supportive and defensive communication.

- To provide participants with an opportunity to create messages that foster supportive and defensive climates.

('94-31)   **511. Let Me:** Introducing Experiential Learning, by J. Allan Tyler (Time required: thirty to thirty-five minutes, plus prework for the facilitator [learning the American Sign Language on the Let Me Illustration Sheet].)

- To acquaint the participants with the concept of experiential learning.

- To demonstrate the positive effects of learning by doing.

COMMUNICATION: Building Trust

(I-90)   **021. Dyadic Encounter:** A Program for Developing Relationships, by John E. Jones and Johanna J. Jones (Time required: a minimum of two hours.)

- To explore knowing and trusting another person through mutual self-disclosure and risk taking.

(I-101)   **022. Nonverbal Communication:** A Collection of Activities (Time required: varies with each activity.)

- To learn new ways of expressing one's feelings, independent of one's vocabulary.

- To express feelings authentically using nonverbal symbolism.

- To focus on nonverbal cues that one emits.

(III-89)   **070. Intimacy Program:** Developing Personal Relationships, adapted from S.M. Jourard (Time required: approximately one and one-half hours.)

- To accelerate the getting-acquainted process in groups.

- To study the experience of self-disclosure.

- To develop authenticity in groups.

(IV-66)   **116. Dialog:** A Program for Developing Work Relationships, by John E. Jones and Johanna J. Jones (Time required: a minimum of two hours.)

- To increase openness in work relationships.

- To generate higher trust in interpersonal relations in work settings.

- To clarify assumptions that people who work together make about one another and one another's jobs.

(IV-96)   **120. Dimensions of Trust:** A Symbolic Expression, by James Costigan (Time required: approximately one hour.)

- To explore the various dimensions and meanings of trust.

- To promote the creative expression of trust.

(V-116)   **169. Dyadic Renewal:** A Program for Developing
                Ongoing Relationships, by Colleen A. Kelley and J.
                Stephen Colladay (Time required: a minimum of two
                hours.)

- To periodically explore various aspects of a
  relationship through mutual self-disclosure and risk
  taking.

('76-46)   **180. Disclosing and Predicting:** A Perception-Checking
                Activity, by Jacques Lalanne (Time required:
                approximately thirty minutes.)

- To aid participants in developing social perception skills.

- To familiarize participants with the concept of
  accurate empathy.

- To demonstrate the effects that first impressions can
  have on perceptions.

('77-57)   **196. Current Status:** A Feedback Activity on Trust, by
                Robert N. Glenn (Time required: approximately one and
                one-half hours.)

- To examine unexpressed feelings of trust or distrust
  within an ongoing group and to clarify the reasons for
  these feelings of trust within the group.

- To promote self-disclosure and risk taking.

- To provide a basis for subsequent assessment of group
  trust.

(VI-130)   **220. Dyadic Risk Taking:** A Perception Check, by Karl C.
                Albrecht and Walton C. Boshear (Time required:
                approximately one hour.)

- To experience the feelings associated with mild
  risk-taking behavior.

- To experiment with controlling the level of risk one is willing to take.

- To experience specific feedback on the degree to which another perceives one's risk.

COMMUNICATION: Conflict

('72-5)   **075. Frustrations and Tensions** (Time required: approximately forty-five minutes.)

- To help participants to become aware of their responses to tense, frustrating situations.

- To study alternative responses to such situations.

('74-22)   **130. Conflict Fantasy:** A Self-Examination, by Joan A. Stepsis (Time required: approximately forty-five minutes.)

- To facilitate awareness of strategies for dealing with conflict situations.

- To examine methods of responding to conflict.

- To introduce the strategy of negotiation and to present the skills required for successful negotiation.

(VI-127)   **219. Escalation:** An Assertion Activity, by Colleen Kelley (Time required: one to two hours.)

- To allow participants to experience success in communicating while under stress.

- To enable participants to practice communicating effectively in stressful situations.

('79-28) **238. Defensive and Supportive Communication:** A Dyadic Role Play, by Gary W. Combs (Time required: approximately one and one-half hours.)

  ▪ To examine the dynamics of defensive and supportive communication in supervisor/subordinate relationships.

  ▪ To develop skills in listening to and understanding a contrasting point of view.

  ▪ To explore the concept of synergy in dyadic communication.

  ▪ To examine the expectations that defensive communication creates for a continuing relationship.

('79-54) **242. Conflict Management:** Dyadic Sharing, by Marc Robert (Time required: approximately one hour.)

  ▪ To identify and share ways of dealing with conflict.

  ▪ To explore new ideas about managing conflict.

(VIII-75) **309. Resistance:** A Role Play, by H.B. Karp (Time required: two to two and one-half hours.)

  ▪ To provide an opportunity to experience the effects of two different approaches to dealing with resistance.

  ▪ To increase awareness of typical responses to attempts to break down resistance.

  ▪ To develop strategies for coping with resistance from others.

('83-80) **340. Conflict Role Play:** Resolving Differences, by Robert P. Belforti, Lauren A. Hagan, Ben Markens, Cheryl A. Monyak, Gary N. Powell, and Karen Sykas Sighinolfi (Time required: approximately two hours.)

- To examine individuals' reactions to situations in which a "double standard" of behavior operates.

- To allow participants to explore their emotional responses to conflict.

- To examine the problem-solving behavior of participants in conflict situations in which a power difference exists.

(IX-84)   **352. The Company Task Force:** Dealing with Disruptive Behavior, by Susanne W. Whitcomb (Time required: two and one-half hours.)

- To help the participants to become aware of the roles and behaviors that are disruptive in meetings, the degree to which they are disruptive, and the positive as well as negative consequences associated with each.

- To offer the participants an opportunity to develop strategies for dealing with disruptive roles and behaviors.

(X-80)   **400. The Decent but Pesky Coworker:** Developing Contracting Skills, by Larry Porter (Time required: approximately one and one-half hours.)

- To acquaint the participants with the significance and usefulness of contracting as a means of facilitating the helping process.

- To develop the participants' understanding of and skills in contracting.

('88-43)   **441. VMX Productions, Inc.:** Handling Resistance Positively, by H.B. Karp (Time required: one hour and twenty minutes to one and one-half hours.)

- To increase the participants' understanding of resistance.

- To provide an opportunity for the participants to explore and compare strategies for dealing with resistance.

- To present the participants with a positive and effective method for handling resistance.

('91-27)   **475. Quality Customer Service:** When the Going Gets Tough, by Bonnie Jameson (Time required: one and one-half to two hours.)

- To increase the participants' understanding of customer behaviors.

- To enhance the participants' awareness of their own responses to customer behaviors.

- To offer the participants an opportunity to share ideas about dealing with difficult customers.

- To help the participants to identify the behaviors that create a positive relationship with customers.

('91-35)   **476. The Parking Space:** Relationships and Negotiating, by Larry Porter (Time required: one and one-half hours.)

- To develop the participants' understanding of the effects of relationships on negotiations.

- To help the participants to become more aware of how changes in roles affect negotiations.

- To help the participants to develop negotiation skills.

('93-19)   **499. Time Flies:** Negotiating Personal Effectiveness Through Assertion, by Michael Lee Smith (Time required: two hours and twenty minutes to two and one-half hours.)

- To demonstrate to the participants the importance of assertive behavior in managing one's time.

- To give the participants an opportunity to practice assertive behavior.

- To give the participants an opportunity to receive feedback about their use of assertion in interpersonal issues that concern time management.

('94-37)   **512. Alpha/Beta:** Exploring Cultural Diversity in Work Teams, by Steven R. Phillips (Time required: approximately two hours.)

- To develop the participants' understanding of the complexities of working in culturally diverse work teams.

- To provide the participants with an opportunity to understand how culturally diverse work teams operate in a simulated environment.

- To encourage the participants to explore the problems and the possibilities that exist in culturally diverse work teams.

COMMUNICATION: Feedback

(I-22)   **006. Group-on-Group:** A Feedback Experience (Time required: approximately one hour.)

- To develop skills in process observation.

- To develop skills in giving appropriate feedback to individual group members.

(I-104)   **023. Coins:** Symbolic Feedback, by J. William Pfeiffer (Time required: approximately one and one-half hours.)

- To experiment with giving feedback symbolically.

- To share feelings involved with giving, receiving, and rejection.

(III-6)   **050. Behavior Description Triads:** Reading Body Language (Time required: approximately fifteen minutes.)

- To practice describing nonverbal behavior objectively, without interpretation.

- To study the body-language messages that accompany verbalization.

- To alert group members to the variety of signals they use to communicate.

('72-58)   **084. Psychomat** (Time required: six to nine hours.)

- To provide an atmosphere in which participants can encounter each other in a variety of ways.

- To encourage creative, sensitive risk taking on the part of participants.

- To explore reactions to a highly unstructured interpersonal situation.

('73-30)   **097. Puzzlement:** A "Mild" Confrontation, by Robert R. Kurtz (Time required: approximately one and one-half hours.)

- To help participants confront each other's behavior in helpful ways.

- To stimulate the amount of feedback given and received in a group.

- To share the feelings involved in giving and receiving feedback.

('73-38)   **099. Analyzing and Increasing Open Behavior:** The Johari Window, by Philip G. Hanson (Time required: approximately two and one-half hours.)

- To describe open and closed behavior in terms of the Johari Window.

- To identify facilitating and inhibiting forces that affect the exchange of feedback.

- To encourage the development of increased open behavior in the group through facilitated feedback.

(IV-15)   **104. The Gift of Happiness:** Experiencing Positive Feedback, by Don Keyworth (Time required: approximately five minutes per participants and about thirty minutes for processing.)

- To promote a climate of trust, self-worth, and positive reinforcement within a small group.

- To experience giving and receiving positive feedback in a nonthreatening way.

(IV-21)   **106. Sculpturing:** An Expression of Feelings, by L.A. McKeown, Beverly Kaye, Richard McLean, and John Linhardt (Time required: approximately forty-five minutes.)

- To provide a nonverbal medium for the expression of feelings toward another person.

- To promote feedback on individual behavior.

(IV-24)   **107. The Portrait Game:** Individual Feedback, by
                 Ferdinand Maire (Time required: a minimum of twenty
                 minutes per participant.)

- To allow participants to receive a composite feedback
  picture from the members of their group as a
  departure from single-source individual feedback.

- To provide an opportunity for participants to compare
  their individual perceptions of how the group is
  experiencing their behavior with the reality of the
  group's experience.

('75-10)   **138. Party Conversations:** A FIRO Role-Play, by Charles L.
                 Kormanski (Time required: approximately two and
                 one-half hours.)

- To experiment with different types of interpersonal
  behavior.

- To demonstrate the concepts in Schutz's theory of
  interpersonal relations.

(V-114)   **168. Adjectives:** Feedback, by John E. Jones (Time
                 required: approximately one hour.)

- To help participants clarify values that apply to human
  relationships.

- To establish the norms of soliciting and giving both
  positive and negative feedback.

(VI-57)   **209. Introspection:** Personal Evaluation and Feedback, by
                 Dennie L. Smith (Time required: approximately forty-five
                 minutes.)

- To provide an opportunity for participants to compare
  their self-assessments with those of others.

('78-34)   **225. Cards:** Personal Feedback, by J. Ryck Luthi (Time required: approximately two hours.)

- To encourage the exchange of personal feedback.

- To provide a means for giving and receiving personal feedback.

(VIII-45)   **303. Developing Trust:** A Leadership Skill, by William J. Bailey (Time required: approximately two hours.)

- To examine some of the behaviors and personal qualities that affect the process of establishing trust in relationships.

- To analyze current behaviors and attitudes related to establishing trust in relationships.

- To increase awareness of how one is perceived by others in regard to behaviors that enhance the building of trust.

(VIII-125)   **315. Giving and Receiving Feedback:** Contracting for New Behavior, by John E. Jones (Time required: approximately three hours.)

- To provide an opportunity for members of a personal-growth group to give and receive feedback on their in-group behavior.

- To enable participants to set behavioral goals for the remainder of the group experience.

(IX-107)   **355. Feedback:** Increasing Self-Perceptions, by Cyril R. Mill (Time required: approximately two hours.)

- To facilitate the process of giving and receiving feedback in a group.

- To help the participants to understand the feedback that they receive.

- To promote a process for exploring the participants' "hidden" characteristics.

(85-11)   **377. Pin Spotter:** Practicing Positive Feedback, by M. Nicholas Mann (Time required: one hour and fifteen minutes.)

- To assist the participants in assessing their abilities to provide feedback.

- To offer the participants an opportunity to practice creating positive feedback statements.

('85-35)   **379. Feedback on Nonverbal and Verbal Behaviors:** Building Communication Awareness, by Gilles L. Talbot (Time required: approximately two hours and forty-five minutes.)

- To enhance the participants' awareness of their own and others' nonverbal and verbal communication patterns.

- To offer the participants an opportunity to give and receive feedback about their communication patterns.

('85-39)   **380. Gaining Support:** Four Approaches, by Juliann Spoth, Barry H. Morris, and Toni C. Denton (Time required: approximately two hours.)

- To acquaint the participants with various approaches to developing individual support within a group.

- To develop the participants' awareness of the positive and negative consequences of these approaches.

(X-8)   **390. I Am, Don't You Think?:** Zodiac Feedback, by Jane C. Bryant (Time required: approximately two hours.)

- To assist the participants in gaining insight about themselves and about their fellow group members.

- To provide the participants with an opportunity to compare their self-perceptions with others' perceptions of them.

- To heighten the participants' awareness of the ways in which a variety of member characteristics can enrich a group.

(X-22)   **391. Two Bags Full:** Feedback About Managerial Characteristics, by Alan R. Carey (Time required: two hours.)

- To offer the participants an opportunity to provide one another with feedback about their managerial traits and behaviors.

- To help each participant to determine his or her strengths and avenues for growth as a manager.

- To assist each participant in developing a set of action steps for personal growth as a manager.

(87-17)   **426. Seeing Ourselves as Others See Us:** Using Video Equipment for Feedback, by Gilles L. Talbot (Time required: approximately one hour, plus an additional ten minutes for each speaker.)

- To enable participants to compare the images they have of themselves with the images they project.

- To increase feedback skills.

- To help participants understand how the differences in self-image and projected image influence interaction.

('89-9)   **449. The Art of Feedback:** Providing Constructive Information, by Stephen C. Bushardt and Aubrey R. Fowler, Jr. (Time required: approximately two and one-half hours.)

- To develop the participants' understanding of how to give and receive feedback.

- To offer the participants an opportunity to practice giving and/or receiving feedback.

- To develop the participants' understanding of the impact of receiving feedback.

- To develop the participants' understanding of how the feedback process can help an individual or a work group to improve functioning.

('92-29)   **487. Feedback Awareness:** Skill Building for Supervisors, by Robert William Lucas (Time required: two hours to two hours and fifteen minutes.)

- To enhance the participants' awareness of the impact of feedback.

- To offer principles and guidelines for giving and receiving feedback.

- To provide a vehicle for practice in giving and receiving feedback.

- To offer the participants an opportunity to discuss and identify feedback characteristics and techniques.

('93-9)   **497. A Note to My Teammate:** Positive Feedback, by Deborah M. Fairbanks (Time required: thirty minutes or less, depending on the size of the group.)

- To provide the participants with an opportunity to experience positive feedback.

- To offer the participants an opportunity to practice giving specific positive feedback.

- To offer the participants a method for improving their working climate.

COMMUNICATION: Listening

(I-31)   **008. Listening Triads:** Building Communications Skills (Time required: approximately forty-five minutes.)

- To develop skills in active listening.

- To study barriers to effective listening.

(II-12)   **028. Rumor Clinic:** A Communications Experiment (Time required: thirty minutes.)

- To illustrate distortions that may occur in transmission of information from an original source through several individuals to a final destination.

(III-10)   **052. Not-Listening:** A Dyadic Role-Play, by Hank B. Karp (Time required: approximately thirty minutes.)

- To allow participants to experience the frustration of not being heard.

- To promote listening readiness.

('73-7)   **087. Peter-Paul:** Getting Acquainted, by Evan L. Solley (Time required: minimum of ten minutes plus two minutes per group member.)

- To help group members get acquainted quickly in a relatively nonthreatening manner.

- To explore feelings generated by "becoming another person."

- To explore the dimensions of a brief encounter.

- To emphasize the need for careful, active listening during conversation.

(VII-39)   **252. Active Listening:** A Communication-Skills Practice, by Jack N. Wismer (Time required: approximately one and one-half hours.)

- To identify the emotional messages that are often hidden in communication.

- To gain practice in active-listening skills.

(X-46)   **395. I'm All Ears:** Enhancing Awareness of Effective Listening, by James I. Costigan and Sandra K. Tyson (Time required: one hour and forty-five minutes.)

- To develop the participants' awareness of some of the requirements for listening effectively.

- To explore the effects of distractions on a person's ability to listen.

('87-25)   **428. Poor Listening Habits:** Identifying and Improving Them, by Joseph Seltzer and Leland Howe (Time required: approximately one and one-half hours.)

- To help participants to identify their poor listening habits.

- To allow participants to practice effective listening skills.

('90-35)   **465. In Reply:** Responding to Feeling Statements, by H. Frederick Sweitzer and Mitchell A. Kosh (Time required: approximately three hours.)

- To offer the participants an opportunity to experience the positive and negative effects that various ways of responding to statements of feelings can have on the sender and the recipient.

- To help the participants to identify their usual patterns of sending and receiving responses to feeling statements and ways in which they might want to alter these patterns.

- To help the participants to identify the responses to statements of feelings that are beneficial to continuing communication.

('94-47)   **513. Needs, Features, and Benefits:** Exploring the Sales Process, by Bonnie Jameson (Time required: one hour and forty-five minutes to two hours.)

- To introduce the concepts of needs, features, and benefits in creating a "case."

- To provide the opportunity for participants to practice writing and presenting needs, features, and benefits.

COMMUNICATION: Styles

('73-20)   **093. Building Open and Closed Relationships,** adapted from William Barber (Time required: one and one-half to two hours.)

- To enable group members to focus on the elements of relationships which characterize them as open or closed.

- To facilitate the cohesiveness of personal growth or otherwise-designated groups who will be working together.

(VI-36) **206. Submission/Aggression/Assertion:** Nonverbal Components, by Gerald N. Weiskott and Mary E. Sparks (Time required: approximately thirty minutes to one hour.)

- To experience and differentiate the nonverbal components of assertive behavior from those of aggressive and submissive (nonassertive) behavior.

- To increase awareness of one's own assertive power.

(VIII-83) **310. Organizational TA:** Interpersonal Communication, by Rich Strand and Frederic R. Wickert (Time required: approximately two hours.)

- To gain insight into the effects on communication of the three ego states: parent (P), adult (A), and child (C).

- To have the experience of operating from each of these three ego states in confrontation situations.

- To acquire skills in observing interactions based on these three ego states.

- To explore the benefits of operating from an adult ego state in confrontation situations.

(X-76) **399. The Human Bank Account:** Practicing Self-Affirmation, based W.C. Boshear and K.G. Albrecht (Time required: two hours.)

- To increase the participants' awareness of their own and others' abilities to affect their self-concepts.

- To offer the participants an opportunity to practice assuming control of their self-concepts and making self-affirming responses to comments made by others.

('89-73)   **457. The Candy Bar:** Using Power Strategies, by Judy H. Farr and Sandra Hagner Howarth (Time required: approximately one and one-half hours.)

- To acquaint the participants with seven bases of power (French & Raven, 1959; Hersey, Blanchard, & Natemeyer, 1979; Raven & Kruglanski, 1975): coercive power, connection power, expert power, information power, legitimate power, referent power, and reward power.

- To offer the participants an opportunity to experience and compare the effects of strategies associated with the seven bases of power.

('93-43)   **503. Stating the Issue:** Practicing "Ownership," by Arthur M. Freedman (Time required: approximately three hours.)

- To present participants with a method for describing personal and organizational issues accurately and specifically.

- To help participants to recognize when and how they may hinder problem solving by disowning responsibility for their part in the issue.

- To offer participants the opportunity to practice the skills needed for non-defensive, open (self-disclosing), and effective communication.

PROBLEM SOLVING: Generating Alternatives

(I-25)   **007. Broken Squares:** Nonverbal Problem-Solving, by
            Tom Isgar (Time required: approximately forty-five
            minutes.)

- To analyze some aspects of cooperation in solving a
  group problem.

- To sensitize participants to behaviors which may
  contribute toward or obstruct the solving of a group
  problem.

(III-14)   **053. Brainstorming:** A Problem-Solving Activity (Time
            required: approximately one hour.)

- To generate an extensive number of ideas or solutions
  to a problem by suspending criticism and evaluation.

- To develop skills in creative problem solving.

('72-11)   **076. Quaker Meeting** (Time required: fifteen minutes for
            the actual "Quaker meeting" plus processing time
            appropriate for the particular group.)

- To generate a large number of ideas, suggestions,
  approaches to a problem or topic when the group is
  too large to employ brainstorming techniques.

- To gather data quickly for a large group to process.

('75-35)   **141. Nominal Group Technique:** An Applied Group
            Problem-Solving Activity, by David L. Ford, Jr. (Time
            required: two hours.)

- To increase creativity and participation in group meetings involving problem-solving and/or fact-finding tasks.

- To develop or expand perception of critical issues within problem areas.

- To identify priorities of selected issues within problems, considering the viewpoints of differently oriented groups.

- To obtain the input of many individuals without the dysfunction of unbalanced participation, which often occurs in large groups.

('77-13) **185. Poems:** Interpersonal Communication, by Brian P. Holleran (Time required: one to one and one-half hours.)

- To experience the interaction conditions necessary for creative problem solving.

- To arrive at a creative solution in a group situation.

('77-35) **192. Package Tour:** Leadership and Consensus Seeking, by Peter Mumford (Time required: approximately two hours.)

- To demonstrate the need for consensus on group goals.

- To demonstrate leadership techniques and strategies in conducting meetings.

- To experience the impact of hidden agendas on group decision making.

('78-9) **221. Numbers:** A Problem-Solving Activity, by Brent D. Ruben and Richard W. Budd (Time required: one to one and one-half hours.)

- To demonstrate how new information and assistance can improve performance.

- To discover how experience facilitates task accomplishment.

('79-41)   **240. Puzzle Cards:** Approaches to Problem Solving, by E.J. (Joe) Cummins (Time required: one to one and one-half hours.)

- To generate an interest in and understanding of different approaches to problem solving.

- To compare advantages and disadvantages of different problem-solving methods.

('81-24)   **285. Analytical or Creative?:** A Problem-Solving Comparison, by Bruce A. McDonald (Time required: approximately one and one-half hours.)

- To provide an opportunity to compare analytical and creative problem-solving approaches.

- To increase awareness of one's own capabilities in and preferences for these two approaches to problem solving.

(VIII-100)   **312. Vacation Schedule:** Group Problem Solving, by L.B. Day and Meeky Blizzard (Time required: approximately two hours.)

- To explore the advantages and disadvantages of using group-decision-making procedures to resolve complex issues.

- To increase awareness of supervisory responsibilities in decision-making situations.

('83-45)   **335. Pebbles:** Vertical and Lateral Problem Solving, by Dan Muller (Time required: approximately one and one-half hours.)

- To provide an opportunity to compare vertical and lateral problem-solving approaches.

- To increase participants' awareness of their preferences for and capabilities in these two approaches to problem solving.

(IX-10)   **343. Bricks:** Creative Problem Solving, by J. Allan Tyler (Time required: approximately one and one-half hours.)

- To provide the participants with an opportunity to practice creative problem solving.

- To allow the participants to experience the dynamics that are involved in group-task accomplishment.

(IX-66)   **350. Departmental Dilemma:** Shared Decision Making, by Janet H. Stevenson (Time required: approximately three hours.)

- To increase the participants' awareness of the process and skills involved in shared decision making.

- To allow the participants to experience shared decision making as a means of conflict management.

('84-44)   **370. QC Agenda:** Collaborative Problem Identification, by Michael J. Miller (Time required: approximately one and one-half hours.)

- To introduce the process by which quality circles identify and select work-related problems as projects.

- To allow the participants to practice behaviors that are associated with effective circle membership: participating collaboratively in circle efforts, listening to other members, and withholding judgment while considering issues that are before the circle.

(X-26)   **392. Water Jars:** Developing Creativity in Problem Solving, by S. Chintamani (Time required: approximately forty-five minutes.)

- To demonstrate the development of mental blocks in problem solving.

- To illustrate that the process of solving problems of a repetitive nature poses a threat to creativity.

- To allow the participants to investigate ways of breaking mental blocks and fostering creative problem solving.

('89-55)   **454. Marzilli's Fine Italian Foods:** An Introduction to Strategic Thinking, by Homer H. Johnson (Time required: approximately one hour and thirty to forty-five minutes.)

- To help the participants to become more aware of the assumptions they make in solving problems.

- To demonstrate the value of suspending assumptions while engaged in problem-solving efforts.

- To introduce the participants to the concept of strategic thinking and to give them an opportunity to practice it.

('90-61)   **467. Cooperative Inventions:** Fostering Creativity, by Robert W. Russell (Time required: approximately forty minutes.)

- To allow the participants to examine their individual approaches to creating ideas.

- To offer the participants an opportunity to share and learn methods of completing a creative task that requires a joint effort.

■ To help the participants to gain insight into factors that inhibit creativity as well as ones that foster creativity.

('90-83)   **470. Greenback Financial Services:** Competitive or Collaborative Problem Solving?, by John E. Hebden (Time required: one and one-half to two hours.)

■ To offer the participants an opportunity to experience a group problem-solving situation.

■ To assist the participants in identifying the feelings evoked by different problem-solving techniques.

■ To help the participants to determine when competition and collaboration are appropriate as problem-solving strategies.

■ To encourage the participants to analyze the effectiveness of their own problem-solving techniques.

('91-97)   **481. Puzzling Encounters:** Creative Brainstorming, by Barbara Harville (Time required: one hour and forty-five minutes.)

■ To help the participants to explore elements of teamwork in group problem solving.

■ To help the participants to explore how to develop creative abilities in a group setting.

■ To provide an opportunity for participants to compare individual creativity with group brainstorming activities.

('93-39)   **502. The Real Meaning:** Creative Problem Solving, by Mary Harper Kitzmiller (Time required: one and one-half hours to two and one-half hours, depending on the size of the group.)

■ To encourage participants to think creatively.

- To help participants identify ways to stimulate creativity.

- To help participants find methods for obtaining creative solutions to problems.

PROBLEM SOLVING: Information Sharing

('72-25)   **080. Energy International:** A Problem-Solving Multiple Role-Play (Time required: approximately two hours.)

- To study how task-relevant information is shared within a work group.

- To observe problem-solving strategies within a group.

- To explore the effects of collaboration and competition in group problem solving.

(IV-75)   **117. Pine County:** Information Sharing, by Lawrence Dunn (Time required: approximately one hour.)

- To explore the effects of collaboration and competition in group problem solving.

- To study how task-relevant information is shared within a work group.

- To observe problem-solving strategies within a group.

- To demonstrate the impact of various leadership styles on task accomplishment.

('74-44)   **133. Farm E-Z:** A Multiple Role Play, Problem-Solving Experience, by Jon L. Joyce (Time required: approximately two hours.)

- To study the sharing of information in task-oriented groups.

- To learn to distinguish a true problem from those which are only symptomatic.

- To observe problem-solving strategies within a group.

(V-34)   **155. Sales Puzzle:** Information Sharing, adapted from Allen A. Zoll III (Time required: approximately one hour.)

- To explore the effects of collaboration and competition in group problem solving.

- To study how information is shared by members of a work group.

- To observe problem-solving strategies within a group.

(V-39)   **156. Room 703:** Information Sharing, by John R. Joachim (Time required: thirty to forty-five minutes.)

- To explore the effects of collaboration and competition in group problem solving.

- To study how task-relevant information is shared within a work group.

- To observe group strategies for problem solving.

('76-26)   **178. Al Kohbari:** An Information-Sharing Multiple Role Play, by Robert E. Mattingly (Time required: approximately two hours.)

- To study how information relevant to a task is shared within work groups.

- To observe problem-solving strategies within work groups.

- To explore the effects of collaboration and competition in group problem solving.

- To demonstrate the effects of hidden agendas on group decision making.

(VI-75)   **212. Murder One:** Information Sharing, by Donald K. McLeod (Time required: one and one-half hours.)

- To explore the effects of cooperation-collaboration versus competition in group problem solving.

- To demonstrate the need for information sharing and other problem-solving strategies in a task-oriented group.

- To study the roles that emerge in a task group.

('81-16)   **284. Farmers:** Information Sharing, by Aharon Kuperman (Time required: approximately two hours.)

- To demonstrate the effects of collaboration and information sharing in problem solving.

- To explore aspects of collaboration such as verbal communication and division of labor.

(IX-125)   **359. The Sales Manager's Journey:** Group Problem Solving, by Guy Fielding (Time required: one and one-half hours.)

- To study the sharing of information in a task-oriented group.

- To examine the various types of member behavior that emerge as a group works on solving a problem.

('85-67)   **383. The Welsh Boothouse:** Intergroup Competition and Collaboration, by Kenneth J. Bowdery (Time required: approximately two and one-half hours.)

- To study the sharing of information in a task-oriented group.

- To examine the types of member and leader behaviors that emerge as a group works on problem solving.

- To demonstrate the effects of competition and collaboration in intergroup relationships.

- To demonstrate the effects of using group representatives as negotiators in intergroup relationships.

('87-57)   **432. Society of Taos:** Group Decision Making, by Michael W. Cooney (Time required: approximately two hours.)

- To allow the participants to experience problem-solving and decision-making strategies within a group.

- To offer the participants an opportunity to study how task-relevant information is shared within a group.

- To demonstrate the effects that individual priorities can have on group decision.

('91-107)   **482. Dust Pan Case:** Solving the Mystery, by Allen E. Dickinson (Time required: one and one-half hours.)

- To help the participants to become aware of the importance of communication and information sharing in groups.

- To develop the participants' awareness of how they share information while completing a task.

- To provide the participants with an opportunity to study how information is shared by members of a group.

('94-55)   **514. Diversity Quiz:** Viewing Differences As Resources, by Linda Eschenburg (Time required: approximately one and one-half hours.)

- To introduce the topic of diversity in the workplace in a nonthreatening way.

- To offer the participants an opportunity to compare the results of individual work with those of group work.

- To give the participants a chance to collaborate with others in order to complete a task.

- To link the concepts of diversity and collaboration.

PROBLEM SOLVING: Consensus/Synergy

(I-49)   **011. Top Problems:** A Consensus-Seeking Task, by John J. Sherwood (Time required: approximately one and one-half hours.)

- To compare the results of individual decision making with the results of group decision making.

- To teach effective consensus-seeking behaviors in task groups.

(I-72)   **015. Residence Halls:** A Consensus-Seeking Task (Time required: approximately one hour.)

- To study the degree to which members of a group agree on certain values.

- To assess the decision making norms of the group.

- To identify the "natural leadership" functioning in the group.

(II-18) **030. NORC:** A Consensus-Seeking Task, by John E. Jones (Time required: approximately one hour.)

- To compare results of individual decision making and of group decision making.

- To generate data to discuss decision-making patterns in task groups.

(III-64) **064. Kerner Report:** A Consensus-Seeking Task (Time required: approximately one hour.)

- To compare the results of individual decision making with the results of group decision making.

- To generate data to discuss decision-making patterns in task groups.

- To diagnose the level of development in a task group.

(III-84) **069. Supervisory Behavior/Aims of Education:** Consensus-Seeking Tasks, adapted from Donald Nylen, J. Robert Mitchell, and Anthony Stout (Time required: approximately one and one-half hours.)

- To explore the relationships between subjective involvement with issues and problem solving.

- To teach effective consensus-seeking behaviors in task groups.

(IV-5) **102. Shoe Store:** Group Problem-Solving, by Amy Zelmer (Time required: thirty to sixty minutes.)

- To observe communication patterns in group problem solving.

- To explore interpersonal influence in problem solving.

(IV-51)   **115. Consensus-Seeking:** A Collection of Tasks, by Don Keyworth, John J. Sherwood, John E. Jones, Tom White, Mary Carson, Bud Rainbow, Ann Dew, Suzanne Pavletich, Ronald D. Jorgenson, and Brant Holmberg (Time required: approximately one hour.)

- To teach effective consensus-seeking behaviors in task groups.

- To explore the concept of synergy in reference to outcomes of group decision making.

('74-64)   **134. Hung Jury:** A Decision-Making Simulation, by Stephen C. Iman, Blake D. Jones, and A. Steven Crown (Time required: approximately two hours.)

- To study decision-making processes.

('74-78)   **135. Kidney Machine:** Group Decision-Making, by Gerald M. Phillips (Time required: approximately one hour.)

- To explore choices involving values.

- To study problem-solving procedures in groups.

- To examine the impact of individuals' values and attitudes on group decision making.

('75-28)   **140. Lost at Sea:** A Consensus-Seeking Task, by Paul M. Nemiroff and William A. Pasmore (Time required: approximately one hour.)

- To teach the effectiveness of consensus-seeking behavior in task groups through comparative experiences with both individual decision making and group decision making.

- To explore the concepts of synergy in reference to the outcomes of group decision making.

(V-10)   **151. Cash Register:** Group Decision Making, based on William V. Haney (Time required: approximately thirty minutes.)

- To demonstrate how decision making is improved by consensus seeking.

- To explore the impact that assumptions have on decision making.

(V-44)   **157. Letter Occurrence/Health Professions Prestige:** Consensus-Seeking Tasks, by Kenneth D. Scott and J. William Pfeiffer (Time required: approximately one hour per task.)

- To compare decisions made by individuals with those made by groups.

- To teach effective consensus-seeking behaviors in task groups.

- To demonstrate the phenomenon of synergy.

('76-19)   **177. Wilderness Survival:** A Consensus-Seeking Task, by Donald T. Simpson (Time required: approximately one and one-half hours.)

- To teach effective consensus-seeking behaviors in task groups.

- To explore the concept of synergy as it relates to outcomes of group decision making.

('77-20)   **187. Pyramids:** A Consensus Experience, by Richard J. Carpenter, Jr. (Time required: approximately two hours.)

- To study the consensus process within an organizational hierarchy.

- To allow participants to define organizational concepts individually and through an organizational process of small-group pyramiding.

- To explore the dynamics of influence and power within groups and organizations.

('78-15)   **223. Admissions Committee:** A Consensus-Seeking Activity, by William J. Heisler (Time required: approximately one and one-half to two hours.)

- To compare decisions made by individuals with those made by groups.

- To teach effective consensus-seeking techniques.

- To teach the concept of synergy.

('79-19)   **236. Alphabet Names:** Achieving Synergy in Task Groups, by Richard P. Greco (Time required: forty-five minutes to one hour.)

- To allow participants to experience the effects of synergy on group tasks.

- To explore the relationship between group commitment to a task and synergy.

('79-71)   **244. What's Important on My Job?:** An Organization Development Activity, by Donald T. Simpson (Time required: one and one-half hours. Additional facilitator time is required to conduct a pre-experience survey and tabulate the results.)

- To examine perceptions about sources of motivation in work situations.

- To experience decision making by group consensus.

(VII-57)   **255. Lists:** A Collection of Consensus Activities, by Barry D. Leskin (Time required: two and one-half to three hours.)

- To allow participants to practice giving and receiving feedback.

- To practice effective consensus-seeking behavior in groups.

- To demonstrate that relevant performance data from interdependent tasks is widely rather than narrowly shared by group members.

('80-20)   **271. Values for the 1980s:** Consensus Seeking, by Leonard D. Goodstein, Warner W. Burke, and Phyliss Cooke (Time required: approximately three hours.)

- To provide an opportunity to explore differences between individual and group decision-making processes.

- To practice consensus-seeking behavior in groups.

- To explore group members' social values.

('87-31)   **429. Ranking Characteristics:** A Comparison of Decision-Making Approaches, by Charles A. LaJeunesse (Time required: one to one and one-half hours.)

- To allow participants to experience three types of decision-making processes: autocratic, democratic, and consensual.

- To demonstrate and compare the relative time required for each of these processes.

- To explore the impacts of each of these approaches on the quality of the decisions, the participants' degree of involvement in the processes, and their preferences for a particular approach.

('93-35)   **501. People Are Electric:** Understanding Heuristics in the Creative Process, by Taggart Smith (Time required: one hour and fifteen minutes to one and one-half hours.)

- To encourage the participants to think creatively.

- To help the participants to discover heuristics in their thinking patterns.

- To assist the participants in recognizing their own selective perception patterns.

- To improve team effectiveness by uncovering judgmental thinking and biases.

PROBLEM SOLVING: Action Planning

(II-79)   **040. Force-Field Analysis:** Individual Problem Solving, based on Warren Bennis and Saul Eisen (Time required: approximately two and one-half hours.)

- To study dimensions of problems and to devise strategies for solving them through diagram and analysis.

- To experience the consultative role.

(III-100)   **073. Wahoo City:** A Role Alternation, by Peter Lawson (Time required: a minimum of two hours.)

- To experience the dynamics of an alternate, unaccustomed role in a situation of community (or organization) conflict.

- To develop skills in conflict resolution, negotiation, and problem solving.

■ To introduce process analysis and feedback as necessary community (or organization) development techniques.

(VII-91)   **259. Dhabi Fehru:** An MBO Activity, by Dwight Bechtel (Time required: three hours.)

■ To examine the process of developing task goals for individuals who are working together on a team project.

■ To provide participants an opportunity to practice writing objectives as part of a Management by Objectives training session.

■ To experience the difference between preparing goals for oneself and for others.

(VII-99)   **260. Island Commission:** Group Problem Solving, by Peter G. Gillan (Time required: one to one and one-half hours.)

■ To experience the issues involved in long-range social planning.

■ To study emergent group dynamics and leadership in the completion of a group task.

■ To explore aspects of communication, problem solving, and decision making in a work group.

('80-43)   **275. Missiles:** Sources of Stress, by Karl A. Seger (Time required: approximately two hours.)

■ To identify sources of psychological stress.

■ To demonstrate the effect that individual perceptions of situations have on behavior and decision making under stress.

- To experience the effects of various types of role power on persons in a decision-making situation.

('83-40)   **334. Robbery:** Planning with PERT, by Mark P. Sharfman and Timothy R. Walters (Time required: one and one-half to two hours.)

- To illustrate the use of the Program Evaluation and Review Technique (PERT) and Critical Path Method (CPM) in planning.

- To allow participants to experience the scheduling and timing of both simultaneous and sequential activities.

- To demonstrate the creation of a basic PERT chart.

('89-83)   **458. The Impact Wheel:** An Empowerment Experience, by Bill Searle (Time required: approximately one hour and forty-five minutes to two hours, depending on the number of subgroups.)

- To help the participants to see ways in which they can empower themselves to affect their work lives.

- To provide the participants with a useful tool for identifying the effects and ramifications of events in their work lives.

- To offer the participants an opportunity to use this tool to analyze a particular work-related event.

- To enable the participants to experience the variety of perspectives that people can have on the same event and to use those different perspectives productively.

('92-9)   **485. Coping Strategies:** Managing Stress Successfully, by Anthony M. Gregory (Time required: approximately one and one-half hours.)

- To offer the participants an opportunity to identify their own patterns of response to stressful situations.

- To assist the participants in identifying thoughts, feelings, and behaviors that help and hinder in coping with stress.

- To encourage the participants to generate alternatives for reducing their self-defeating reactions to stress and for enhancing the positive reactions that lead to successful outcomes.

('94-67)   **515. Wreck Survivors:** Operating from Strategic Assumptions, by Virginia Prosdocimi (Time required: two hours to two hours and twenty minutes.)

- To explore common patterns found in group problem solving and consensus seeking.

- To enable participants to practice clarifying strategic assumptions.

- To identify the differences between "strategy" and "tactics."

GROUPS: How Groups Work

(I-36)   **009. Committee Meeting:** Demonstrating Hidden Agendas, by Jerry Gold and Len Miller (Time required: approximately one and one-half hours.)

- To illustrate the effects of hidden agendas on task accomplishment in a work group.

(I-45)   **010. Process Observation:** A Guide (Time required: minimum of ten minutes for processing.)

- To provide feedback to a group concerning its process.

- To provide experience for group members in observing process variables in group meetings.

(II-16)   **029. Group Tasks:** A Collection of Activities (Time
required: varies with each activity.)

- To be used in studying group process.

(II-68)   **037. Self-Interaction-Task:** Process Observation Guides,
by John E. Jones (Time required: two hours.)

- To practice observing small-group process.

- To gain experience in reporting process observations
to a group.

- To provide instrumental feedback on one's
interpersonal orientations.

(III-17)   **054. Towers:** An Intergroup Competition (Time
required: approximately one and one-half hours.)

- To study phenomena of competition among groups.

- To explore the feeling content and behavioral
outcomes of winning and losing.

- To provide a basis for feedback to group members on
their relations with other group members and their
productivity in a task situation.

('72-19)   **079. What To Look for in Groups:** An Observation
Guide, by Philip G. Hanson (Time required: three hours.)

- To assist group members in understanding and being
more perceptive about group process.

('72-44)   **082. Greeting Cards:** An Organization Simulation (Time
required: three to six hours.)

- To observe a group's organizational style and
functioning.

■ To gather data on individuals' responses to creating and operating a production-centered organization.

■ To give group members feedback on their organizational behavior.

('74-8)   **126. Cog's Ladder:** A Process-Observation Activity, by George O. Charrier (Time required: one hour.)

■ To enhance awareness of factors which distinguish process from content in group interaction.

■ To explore a model of group development.

('75-15)   **139. Faculty Meeting:** A Multiple Role-Play, by Frederick H. McCarty and Bernard Nisenholz (Time required: approximately two and one-half hours.)

■ To study behaviors that facilitate and that block communication in groups.

■ To explore the effects of process feedback on team functioning.

(V-60)   **160. Tinkertoy® Bridge:** Intergroup Competition, by Geoff Bellman (Time required: approximately one and one-half hours.)

■ To analyze individual and team actions in relation to on-the-job experiences.

■ To build awareness of the need for teamwork in completing a task.

■ To demonstrate the effects of competition on team efforts.

(V-73)   **161. LEGO® Bridge:** Intergroup Competition, by Peter
            Mumford (Time required: approximately one and
            one-half hours.)

            ■ To observe spontaneous patterns of organization in
              work groups.

            ■ To explore the relationship between planning and
              production.

            ■ To study the effects of intergroup competition on team
              functioning.

(VI-15)   **200. Word-Letter:** A Problem-Solving Activity, by Jordan
            P. Berliner (Time required: approximately one and
            one-half hours.)

            ■ To demonstrate how problems are resolved when the
              alternatives are not clearly defined or the situation is
              ambiguous.

            ■ To explore group problem-solving processes.

(VI-117)   **218. Spy:** An Intergroup Activity, by Stephen J. Schoen
            (Time required: approximately one and one-half hours.)

            ■ To explore the impact of competition between groups.

            ■ To demonstrate different methods of group problem
              solving.

            ■ To examine the dynamics of suspicion and distrust in a
              group.

            ■ To observe the process of a leaderless group in the
              completion of a specific task.

('78-46)   **228. Homesell:** Intergroup Competition, by Joel
            Zimmerman (Time required: approximately three hours.
            May be conducted in two sessions of one and one-half
            hours each.)

- To explore the ways in which members interact in a work group.

- To demonstrate different methods of group problem solving.

- To relate members' group behavior to back-home situations.

('79-21) **237. Line of Four:** An Intergroup Competition, by William R. Mulford (Time required: approximately one and one-half hours.)

- To examine a group's communication, planning, and collaborative behavior.

- To examine the use of self-imposed rules of behavior.

- To explore the dynamics of intergroup competition.

(VII-69) **256. Slingshots:** Studying Group Dynamics, by Kenneth M. Bond (Time required: approximately one hour and fifteen minutes.)

- To experience the group dynamics involved in task accomplishment.

- To study the effects of competition on group functioning.

- To experience the functional and dysfunctional aspects of process interventions.

('81-34) **287. Four-Letter Words:** Examining Task-Group Processes, by Walter J. Cox (Time required: approximately two and one-half hours.)

- To study the behavior of an unstructured group in accomplishing a complex task.

- To heighten awareness of the importance of correct interpretation of written task instructions.

- To enable group members to compare observed behavior with typical task-group behavior.

- To assist group members to better perceive and understand individual interactions within a task group.

('81-50)   **290. Dynasell:** Hidden Agendas and Trust, by William W. Kibler (Time required: one and one-half to two hours.)

- To demonstrate the impact of distrust on collaboration in a task group.

- To heighten awareness of one's personal responses when the motives of others are in question.

(VIII-69)   **308. Structures:** Intergroup Competition, by Anthony C. Stein, Stephen C. Iman, and Albert A. Ramos (Time required: approximately two hours.)

- To study the effects of intergroup competition on group processes.

- To identify helps and hindrances to task accomplishment.

- To demonstrate the impact of effective and ineffective communication processes in task groups.

(IX-74)   **351. Team Planning:** Effects of Differential Information, by Thomas J. Mallinson, Ron Sept, and Alan Tolliday (Time required: approximately two hours.)

- To explore the dynamics of team planning.

- To examine the differences in communication, planning, and collaboration behavior when teams are given different amounts of information as the basis for completing a task.

(IX-114)   **357. Group Sell:** Advertising Group Values, by Tim A. Flanagan (Time required: one and one-half to two hours.)

- To explore the participants' reasons for joining groups and the attractiveness of different types of groups.

- To examine issues concerning group loyalties and values about groups.

('88-51)   **442. Four Corners:** Preferences That Affect Group Work, by Bonnie Jameson (Time required: approximately one hour.)

- To acquaint the participants with the four essential elements of group work.

- To explain how these elements interact and how people's preferences for particular elements affect group functioning.

- To provide an opportunity for the participants to increase their awareness of which of the four elements they prefer, which their organizations prefer, and the implications of these preferences.

('88-57)   **443. Orientations:** Left-Brain/Right-Brain Problem Solving, by Daniel C. Nacht, Kurt Kraiger, and Ruth Mandrell (Time required: approximately two hours.)

- To acquaint the participants with the basic theory of left-brain and right-brain orientations.

- To provide a way for each participant to determine his or her particular orientation.

- To examine the ways in which different orientations affect the completion of group tasks.

- To develop the participants' understanding of the benefits and drawbacks of their own and others' orientations.

('92-63)   **491. Whirlybird:** Examining Competition and Collaboration, by Gary Gemmill and Gary Wagenheim (Time required: one hour and fifteen to thirty minutes.)

- To offer the participants an opportunity to experience and explore both intragroup collaboration and intergroup competition.

- To encourage the participants' creativity.

- To facilitate team building within individual subgroups through the completion of a collaborative task.

GROUPS: Competition/Collaboration

(II-29)   **032. Model-Building:** An Intergroup Competition (Time required: approximately one and one-half hours.)

- To study interpersonal and intergroup competition phenomena.

- To explore the feeling content and behavioral results of winning and losing.

- To provide feedback to group members on their contributions in a task situation.

(III-52)   **061. Prisoners' Dilemma:** An Intergroup Competition (Time required: approximately one hour.)

- To explore trust between group members and effects of betrayal of trust.

- To demonstrate effects of interpersonal competition.

- To dramatize the merit of a collaborative posture in intragroup and intergroup relations.

('72-51) **083. Decisions:** An Intergroup Negotiation, by Henry I. Feir with Richard J. Turner, Robert Cox, Daniel N. Kanouse, and Robert G. Mason (Time required: a minimum of four and one-half hours.)

- To experience the issues surrounding intergroup trust building and trust betrayal.

- To explore considerations of intergroup competition versus collaboration.

- To examine limited communication under stress.

- To study negotiation and negotiation strategies.

- To consider group decision-making processes.

(IV-18) **105. Wooden Blocks:** A Competition Exercise, by Amy Zelmer (Time required: approximately one hour.)

- To explore individual and small group goal-setting behavior and achievement motivation.

- To study interpersonal and intergroup competition phenomena.

- To explore feelings and outcomes of winning and losing.

('75-56) **147. World Bank:** An Intergroup Negotiation, by Norman H. Berkowitz and Harvey A. Hornstein (Time required: approximately three hours.)

- To experience the conflict between advantages of cooperation and advantages of competition in a mixed-motive dilemma.

- To explore some dynamics of trust between groups.

- To practice negotiation skills.

(V-91)   **164. Testing:** Intergroup Competition, by Peter R. Scholtes (Time required: approximately one and one-half hours.)

- To explore the impact of the lack of communication in competitive situations.

- To demonstrate the need for collaboration and interdependence.

('76-41)   **179. X-Y:** A Three-Way Intergroup Competition, by Gustave J. Rath, Jeremy Kisch, and Holmes E. Miller (Time required: approximately two hours.)

- To explore interpersonal trust.

- To demonstrate the effects of cooperation, competition, and betrayal.

- To dramatize the advantages of both competitive and collaborative models in intergroup relations.

('77-24)   **189. Blue/Green:** An Intergroup Negotiation, adapted from James Owens (Time required: one and one-half hours.)

- To explore the element of trust between group members and the effects of the betrayal of trust.

- To demonstrate the effects of competition and collaboration in intergroup relationships.

- To study the effects of win-lose, win-win, and lose-lose strategies in negotiations between groups.

(VI-32)   **205. Circle in the Square:** A Cooperation/Competition Activity, by Clyde E. Lee (Time required: approximately one hour.)

■ To demonstrate how cooperation and competition can affect winning and losing.

■ To explore how winning and losing are defined, perceived, and measured.

('78-63)   **231. Balance of Power:** A Cooperation/Competition Activity, by Lucian Parshall (Time required: approximately two and one-half hours.)

■ To explore the effects of collaboration and competition strategies in group problem solving.

■ To study how task-relevant information is shared between groups.

■ To increase awareness of the influence that leaders (or political systems) have on decision making in groups.

('79-60)   **243. Paper Box:** An Intergroup-Competition Activity, by James G. Clawson (Time required: two and one-half to three hours.)

■ To study intra- and inter-group relations and conflict.

■ To demonstrate the effects of collaboration versus those of competition.

■ To demonstrate the impact of negotiation on collaborative activities.

■ To practice intragroup planning and problem-solving processes.

(VII-112)   **263. Trading Cards:** A Power Simulation, by Jay Proescher (Time required: one and one-half to two hours.)

- To experience the consequences of conflict between group goals and goals of individual members.

- To experience intergroup and intragroup competition.

- To identify patterns of competition and cooperation among group members in a stressful situation.

- To identify how group and individual strategies affect the group's attainment of a goal.

(VII-117)   **264. War Gaming:** An Intergroup Competition, by Allen J. Schuh (Time required: two to four hours.)

- To study group decision making and interaction under stress.

- To examine the importance of cooperation in small-group work.

- To demonstrate the effects of win-win and win-lose approaches to intergroup conflict.

('80-60)   **278. Move to Newtown:** A Collaboration Activity, by Richard Parker and Annette A. Hartenstein (Time required: a minimum of three hours.)

- To increase awareness of the dynamics of competition and collaboration.

- To experience the effects of the use of role power in negotiation situations.

- To explore the effects of role expectations on behavior and reactions.

■ To practice renegotiation of role responsibilities and expectations within a work unit.

('80-78)　　**280. High Iron:** Collaboration and Competition, by Donald T. Simpson (Time required: approximately two hours.)

■ To examine the elements of negotiation and collaboration in achieving goals.

■ To experience the effects of collaboration and/or competition in problem solving.

(VIII-41)　　**302. Cross-Group Negotiation and Cooperation:** Studying Group Dynamics, by Barbara L. Fisher and Roberta G. Sachs (Time required: approximately one and one-half hours.)

■ To provide an opportunity to experience the effects of cooperation in task-group functioning.

■ To explore the effects of conflicting objectives on the behavior of members of a task group.

■ To increase awareness of the positive effects of planning, negotiation, and sharing of resources among work-group members.

(VIII-93)　　**311. Risk Game:** Competition and Team Building, by Allen J. Schuh (Time required: approximately two hours.)

■ To increase awareness of one's preferred level of risk taking.

■ To increase awareness of how the attitudes of others can affect one's choices and level of risk taking.

■ To study the effects of intergroup competition on intragroup communication processes.

('82-20)   **319. Intertwine:** Intergroup Collaboration, by Marshall Sashkin (Time required: approximately one and one-half to two hours.)

- To illustrate intergroup task interdependence.

- To explore aspects of collaboration such as communication and division of labor.

- To practice intergroup problem-solving skills.

('82-24)   **320. Block Buster:** A Collaboration Activity, by R. Moses Thompson (Time required: one and one-half to two hours.)

- To experience elements of teamwork in group problem solving.

- To examine the effects of planning on task achievement.

- To examine the significance of communication and rhythm in a particular type of group task.

('85-75)   **384. Stock Exchange:** A Collaborative Activity, by Kenneth W. Howard (Time required: one hour and forty minutes.)

- To provide the participants with an opportunity to experience the effects of different approaches to developing resources.

- To develop the participants' awareness of the advantages and disadvantages of various collaborative strategies.

('94-75)   **516. Assignment Flexibility:** Comparing Negotiation Styles, by John E. Oliver (Time required: two hours and forty-five minutes.)

- To allow participants to experience the "hardball" negotiation process.

- To allow participants to practice the "win-win" negotiation process.

- To allow participants to compare the effects of "hardball" negotiation and "win-win" negotiation.

- To provide information about "assignment flexibility" and its perceived advantages and disadvantages in work negotiations.

GROUPS: Conflict

(I-70)   **014. Conflict Resolution:** A Collection of Tasks (Time required: varies with each activity.)

- To generate data about how groups resolve conflict.

('75-46)   **144. Lindell-Billings Corporation:** A Confrontation Role-Play, by Thomas H. Patten, Jr. (Time required: approximately three hours.)

- To provide an opportunity to practice confrontation.

- To explore design considerations in using confrontation inside an organization.

- To examine and develop skills in intergroup conflict, negotiation, and problem solving.

('77-15)   **186. Conflict Styles:** Organizational Decision Making, by Donald T. Simpson (Time required: approximately one and one-half hours.)

- To identify ways of dealing with organizational or group conflict.

- To discuss when and why different methods of resolving conflict are appropriate to different situations.

- To provide an experience in group decision making.

('78-28)   **224. Controversial Issues:** Case Studies in Conflict, by Julia T. Wood (Time required: approximately one and one-half to two hours.)

- To examine the effects of conflict on members of problem-solving groups.

- To acquaint members with alternative methods of coping with conflict in groups.

- To examine individual styles of handling conflicts and their effects among members of problem-solving groups.

('82-35)   **323. Budget Cutting:** Conflict and Consensus Seeking, by Terry L. Maris (Time required: approximately two and one-half hours.)

- To experience the dynamics of consensus seeking in a decision-making group.

- To provide experience in establishing priorities.

- To explore methods for resolving conflict in decision-making groups.

- To examine individual ways of handling conflict in groups.

('84-67)   **374. Trouble in Manufacturing:** Managing Interpersonal Conflict, by John E. Oliver (Time required: approximately one and one-half hours.)

- To examine ways of managing interpersonal conflict in an organizational setting.

- To provide the participants with an opportunity to practice conflict management.

('84-74)   **375. Datatrak:** Dealing with Organizational Conflict, by David J. Foscue and Kenneth L. Murrell (Time required: two to two and one-half hours.)

- To illustrate the types of conflict that can arise within a work group.

- To provide the participants with an opportunity to experience and deal with organizational conflict.

- To help the participants to identify effective and ineffective methods of resolving conflict.

('87-79)   **435. Winterset High School:** An Intergroup-Conflict Simulation, by Charles E. List (Time required: approximately two and one-half hours.)

- To provide participants with an opportunity to practice a conflict-management strategy.

- To examine ways that occupational stereotyping can contribute to organizational conflict.

GROUPS: Negotiating/Bargaining

('72-17)   **078. Unequal Resources** (Time required: approximately one hour.)

- To provide an opportunity for observing group use of resources which have been distributed unequally.

- To observe bargaining processes.

(VII-124)   **265. Monetary Investment:** Negotiation, by Tom Armor (Time required: one and one-half to two hours.)

- To provide insight into the dynamics of negotiation processes: strategy, constituent pressure, consensus, and mediation.

- To simulate a collective bargaining experience.

- To explore the behavior of participants in a bargaining situation.

('80-69)   **279. Creative Products:** Intergroup Conflict Resolution, by William J. Heisler and Robert W. Shively (Time required: two and one-half to three hours.)

- To examine the effects of collaboration and competition in intergroup relationships.

- To demonstrate the effects of win-win and win-lose approaches to intergroup conflict.

- To practice intragroup planning and problem solving.

(VIII-120)   **314. Territory:** Intergroup Negotiation, by Phyliss Cooke and Anthony J. Reilly (Time required: approximately two and one-half hours.)

- To experience the effects of a negotiation activity.

- To increase awareness of various negotiation strategies.

- To practice collaboration strategies in intergroup problem solving.

('90-95)   **471. Bargaining, United Nations Style:** Exploring the Impact of Cultural Values, by Julia T. Oliver and John E. Oliver (Time required: approximately two to two and one-half hours.)

- To offer each participant an opportunity to experience being a person from a different culture.

- To offer the participants an opportunity to interact with people who represent a different culture.

- To demonstrate the effects of cultural differences on interactions between members of different cultures.

- To allow the participants to experience the process of negotiation between two people whose values differ.

TEAMS: How Groups Work

(IV-38) **111. System Problems:** A Diagnostic Activity, by Morton S. Perlmutter (Time required: approximately one hour.)

- To generate data about the functioning of an intact group or a growth group.

- To diagnose the way a system approaches problem solving.

('77-47) **194. Top Secret Contract:** Intergroup Model Building, by Robert W. Landies and Tom Isgar (Time required: approximately two and one-half hours.)

- To provide a developing or an intact team an experience in the use of newly acquired skills in leadership style, problem solving, decision making, and communication processes.

- To study group dynamics in a task situation: competition/collaboration, negotiation, confrontation/avoidance, etc.

- To point out the effect that external influences (outside agents, competition built into the system, production requirements, time and other constraints, etc.) have on team task accomplishment and on individual team members.

(VI-54)   **208. Team Development:** A TORI Model, by Gary R. Gemmill (Time required: approximately two and one-half hours.)

- To study TORI growth processes.

- To practice applying a theoretical model to group self-diagnosis.

('80-51)   **276. Slogans:** A Group-Development Activity, by Suresh M. Sant (Time required: approximately three hours.)

- To experience the processes and feelings that arise when a new member joins an ongoing group with defined tasks and roles.

- To explore the coping mechanisms adopted by the individual and the group to deal with entry problems.

- To examine functional and dysfunctional coping strategies of groups.

('81-43)   **288. Project Colossus:** Intragroup Competition, by James V. Fee (Time required: one to one and one-half hours.)

- To explore the dynamics of status, power, and special knowledge in decision making.

- To examine the effects of intragroup competition on team functioning.

(VIII-25)   **299. Group Identity:** A Developmental Planning Session, by Kenneth W. Howard (Time required: approximately two hours.)

- To provide the members of an intact group with a model for understanding the factors that influence its development.

- To enable the members of an intact group to identify its current stage of growth.

- To promote group cohesiveness by exploring the needs and interests of its members.

('82-31)   **322. Chips:** Agenda Building, by Charles A. Hill, Jr., and Edward L. Emerson (Time required: one and one-half to two hours, plus prework.)

- To select agenda items that have the highest value to the members of an intact group.

- To promote awareness of the agenda items of others and the degree of commitment to those items.

- To promote synergy in the group by means of negotiation.

('82-49)   **325. Meetings Audit:** Planning for Improvement, by H. Kent Baker (Time required: two hours.)

- To practice group planning and problem solving.

- To provide an opportunity for the members of an intact group to provide feedback about their meetings.

- To generate commitment to specific suggestions for improving the meetings of an intact group.

('82-60)   **327. Work-Group Review:** Team Building, by Allen J. Schuh (Time required: four and one-half hours, plus prework.)

- To provide an opportunity for open communication in an intact work group.

- To stimulate discussion between coworkers in the same work setting.

- To heighten awareness of coworkers' attitudes about work-related topics.

- To identify topics of concern collaboratively for further consideration and review by the organization.

(X-96)   **404. Healthy or Unhealthy?:** Assessing Group Functioning (Time required: approximately two hours and fifteen minutes.)

- To offer the participants an opportunity to assess the health of their group in terms of functional and dysfunctional member behaviors and to provide the group with feedback about this assessment.

- To assist the participants in developing a group definition of a "healthy" group and an "unhealthy" group.

- To help the participants to establish action steps to take to improve their group's functioning.

(X-99)   **405. Sticky Wickets:** Exploring Group Stress, by William B. Kline and Joseph J. Blase (Time required: one hour and forty-five minutes to two hours.)

- To develop the participants' awareness of the factors that can lead to group stress.

- To allow the participants to experience some of these factors.

- To offer the participants an opportunity to share with one another their ideas for dealing with group stress.

('86-45)   **419. Bean Bags:** Leadership and Group Development, by Derrick Suehs and Florence Rogers (Time required: one to one and one-half hours.)

- To allow the participants to experience the effects of leadership behavior on a task group.

- To demonstrate how changes in task, the addition/deletion of staff, and managerial style affect the development and performance of a work group.

('87-75)   **434. Instant Survey:** Creating Agenda for Team Building, by Charles A. Cotton (Time required: from one and one-half to two hours.)

- To generate working agenda for a meeting in which the participants will discuss their concerns about work-group issues that will face them in the future.

- To determine in a nonthreatening way the hidden needs and concerns of the participants.

- To present for discussion the concerns of all the participants.

- To provide participants with a method for creating participant-owned, meaningful agenda that will assist facilitators in designing team-building sessions for the participants.

TEAMS: Roles

(II-72) **038. Role Nominations:** A Feedback Experience, based on K. Benne and P. Sheats (Time required: approximately one and one-half hours.)

- To provide feedback to group members on the roles fellow members see them playing.

- To study various types of roles in relation to group goals.

- To demonstrate that leadership in a small group consists of several functions which should be shared among members.

(III-46) **059. Line-Up and Power Inversion:** An Experiment (Time required: approximately one and one-half hours.)

- To expand the individual's awareness of his influence on the group.

- To experience power inversion.

(V-136) **171. Role Clarification:** A Team-Building Activity, by John E. Jones (Time required: a minimum of three hours.)

- To clarify both expectations that team members have of others' roles and conceptions that team members have of their own roles.

- To promote renegotiation of role responsibilities within a work unit.

- To teach a process of role adjustment that can become a work group norm.

('80-14)   **270. Baseball Game:** Group-Membership Functions, by Robert W. Rasberry (Time required: approximately three hours.)

- To gain insight into how one is perceived by others.

- To study the variety of functions performed by group members.

- To introduce a novel way of characterizing group-member roles.

('82-55)   **326. The Car:** Feedback on Group Membership Styles, by Alfred A. Wells (Time required: approximately one and one-half hours.)

- To allow the members of an ongoing work group to obtain feedback on their perceived role functions and membership styles.

- To enable a group to examine its operating style and to plan changes.

- To encourage and practice giving and receiving feedback.

('84-16)   **366. The Seven Pieces:** Identifying Group Roles, by Nadine J. (Hoffman) Carpenter (Time required: approximately one hour.)

- To introduce participants to roles that emerge in a group.

- To provide the participants with an opportunity to experience and assume some of these roles and to observe their impact on the group process.

('84-26)   **368. Role Power:** Understanding Influence, by Patrick Doyle (Time required: approximately two hours.)

- To explore the types of power inherent in different roles in group settings.

- To acquaint the participants with various power strategies that can be used in a decision-making process.

- To help the participants to develop an understanding of effective and ineffective uses of power.

(X-122)   **408. Kaleidoscope:** Team Building Through Role Expansion, by Carlo E. Cetti and Mary Kirkpatrick Craig (Time required: two hours and twenty minutes to approximately six hours.)

- To allow members of a team to clarify their roles and to give and receive feedback about their existing and potential contributions to the team.

- To promote team building through self-disclosure, feedback, and commitment among team members.

- To widen the team members' views of one another's abilities and valuable qualities.

('86-51)   **420. Position Power:** Exploring the Impact of Role Change, by Phyliss Cooke and Lawrence C. Porter (Time required: approximately three hours.)

- To explore the effects of power and status on attitudes and performance.

- To become more aware of how changes in the roles of task-group members affect attitudes and performance.

('89-61)   **455. America's Favorite Pastime:** Clarifying Role Perceptions, by Tim Hildebrandt (Time required: one hour and forty-five minutes to two hours.)

- To identify the various roles that exist in a team.

- To provide a means for sharing the team members' perceptions of their roles.

- To develop the members' awareness of their own contributions to the team as well as the contributions of fellow team members.

- To assist the team members in identifying ways to use their perceptions of their own and one another's roles to improve team functioning.

('90-73)   **469. Symbols:** Sharing Role Perceptions, by Patrick Doyle (Time required: approximately one hour and fifteen minutes.)

- To familiarize the participants with the various roles that exist in a work team.

- To provide the participants with the opportunity to share perceptions of their roles in their work team.

- To provide the participants with the opportunity to practice giving and receiving feedback.

('91-85)   **480. Multiple Roles:** Nature and Orientation, by Manish Nandy (Time required: approximately two hours.)

- To develop the participants' awareness of multiple roles in groups.

- To offer participants a system for categorizing the nature and orientation of group roles.

- To offer participants the opportunity to determine ways to improve group functioning in the future.

('93-31)   **500. Yours, Mine, and Ours:** Clarifying Team Responsibilities, by Mike M. Milstein (Time required: approximately three to three and one-half hours for a group with five or six members. The facilitator should add or subtract ten minutes for each member above or below that number.)

- To assist the participants in clarifying and establishing agreements about which activities are their group's responsibilities and which are the responsibility of individual members (including the formal leader).

TEAMS: Problem Solving/Decision Making

(II-24)   **031. Lutts and Mipps:** Group Problem-Solving, based on Rimoldi (Time required: approximately forty-five minutes.)

- To study the sharing of information in a task-oriented group.

- To focus on cooperation in group problem solving.

- To observe the emergence of leadership behavior in group problem solving.

(IV-8)   **103. Joe Doodlebug:** Group Problem-Solving, adapted from Milton Rokeach (Time required: approximately forty-five minutes.)

- To explore the effect of participants' response sets in a group problem-solving activity.

- To observe leadership behavior in a problem-solving situation.

('74-32)   **132. Planning Recommendations or Action:** A Team-Development Guidebook, by Robert P. Crosby (Time required: approximately three hours.)

- To study the process of group decision making.

- To explore action planning.

('83-65)   **337. The Lawn:** Problem or Symptom?, by William W. Kibler and William T. Milburn (Time required: approximately one and one-half hours.)

- To provide an experience in clearly defining a problem.

- To increase awareness of the difference between the causes of a problem and the symptoms of a problem.

- To demonstrate how using only oral communication can affect the problem-solving process.

('84-62)   **373. Threats to the Project:** A Team-Building Activity, by Donald T. Simpson (Time required: approximately one hour and forty-five minutes.)

- To increase the participants' understanding of group dynamics.

- To enhance the participants' effectiveness as team members.

('87-51)   **431. Unscrambling the Bank Accounts:** Group Problem Solving, by John E. Hebden (Time required: approximately one hour.)

- To enable participants to experience group problem-solving processes.

- To give participants an opportunity to observe and identify behaviors and methods that facilitate or hinder effective teamwork.

- To highlight the consequences of conflicts between individual objectives and team objectives.

- To provide a basis for exploring means to make teamwork more effective.

('89-47)   **453. Control or Surrender:** Altering Approaches to Problem Solving, by Jim Ballard (Time required: approximately one hour and forty minutes.)

- To introduce the participants to a method for changing the way in which they perceive problems.

- To assist the participants in developing action plans in which they apply their changed perceptions to a group-owned problem.

- To assist the participants in synthesizing their individual action plans into a group approach to dealing with the problem.

TEAMS: Feedback

(I-79)   **017. Leveling:** Giving and Receiving Adverse Feedback, by J. William Pfeiffer (Time required: approximately ten minutes per participant.)

- To let participants compare their perceptions of how a group sees them with the actual feedback obtained from the group.

- To legitimize giving negative feedback within a group.

- To develop skills in giving negative feedback.

(I-82)   **018. Dependency-Intimacy:** A Feedback Experience, by John E. Jones (Time required: approximately one and one-half hours.)

- To provide instrumented feedback.

- To study how the personal dimensions of dependency and intimacy affect group development.

(II-76)   **039. Group Development:** A Graphic Analysis, by John E. Jones (Time required: approximately forty-five minutes.)

- To compare the development of a small group along the dimensions of task functions and personal relations.

- To compare members' perceptions of the developmental status of a group at a given time.

(III-22)   **055. Group Self-Evaluations:** A Collection of Instruments (Time required: varies according to the evaluative procedures used.)

- To help a group evaluate its own functioning.

- To provide a way to examine objectively the participation of group members.

- To explore the norms that have developed in a group which has been meeting for some time.

(III-33)   **057. Nominations:** Personal Instrumented Feedback (Time required: approximately one hour.)

- To provide feedback to group members on how they are perceived by each other.

- To analyze the climate and the norms of the group by studying members' behavior, composition of the group, and members' expectations of each other.

(III-49)   **060. Dividing the Loot:** Symbolic Feedback (Time required: one hour.)

- To provide symbolic feedback to participants.

- To explore the responsibilities and problems of leadership.

(III-73)   **066. Team Building:** A Feedback Experience (Time required: a minimum of one day.)

- To help an intact work group diagnose its functioning.

- To establish a cooperative expectation within a task group.

- To assist a "real life" group or business manager (leader, chairman, supervisor) to develop norms of openness, trust, and interdependence among team members and/or members of his organization.

- To help team members clarify and evaluate their personal goals, the team's goals, and the relationship between these two sets of aims.

(III-78)   **067. Organizational Mirror:** A Feedback Experience (Time required: approximately two hours.)

- To generate data that can permit an organization to diagnose its functioning.

- To establish avenues of feedback between an organization and other groups with which it is linked.

('72-13)   **077. Team Identity,** by John E. Jones (Time required: approximately one and one-half hours.)

- To develop cohesion within work groups established as part of a larger training group.

- To explore the dynamics of group task accomplishment.

(IV-88) **118. Twenty-Five Questions:** A Team Development Exercise, by John E. Jones (Time required: approximately one and one-half hours.)

- To enhance work relationships in intact groups.

- To stimulate group discussion about work-related topics.

- To clarify assumptions that team members make about each other.

(V-108) **166. Agenda Setting:** A Team-Building Starter, by John E. Jones (Time required: approximately one hour.)

- To create and rank-order an agenda for a team-building session.

- To generate ownership of and commitment to commonly perceived problems facing a work group.

- To develop effective listening skills.

(V-111) **167. Cups:** A Power Experience, by Anthony J. Reilly (Time required: approximately two hours.)

- To increase awareness of the meanings of power.

- To experience giving, receiving, and not receiving power.

(V-131) **170. Person Perception:** Feedback, by Robert H. Dolliver (Time required: approximately one hour.)

- To provide feedback to individual group members about how they are perceived by others.

- To help participants clarify what underlies their tendency to categorize other people.

(VI-110)   **216. Affirmation of Trust:** A Feedback Activity, by Brian
              P. Holleran (Time required: approximately two hours.)

- To increase understanding of physical, intellectual,
  and emotional trust.

- To explore how the trust level existing in the group
  affects the openness of discussion.

- To provide an opportunity for group members to give
  one another feedback on trust.

(VII-53)   **254. Stones, Bands, and Circle:** Sociogram Activities, by
              Donald E. Miskiman, John E. Hoover, Melvin A.
              Goldstein, and Donald Anderson (Time required:
              approximately forty-five minutes to one hour per activity.)

- To explore existing levels of interaction, influence,
  and inclusion in a group.

- To develop an awareness of group dynamics.

('81-54)   **291. I Hear That You...:** Giving and Receiving Feedback,
              by Drew P. Danko and Rich Cherry (Time required: one
              and one-half to two hours.)

- To establish a climate conducive to giving and
  receiving feedback in established work groups.

- To practice active listening and feedback skills.

- To help make work-group behavior more
  understandable by linking behavior to perceptions.

- To improve work-group relations and climate.

(VIII-18)   **297. Group Effectiveness:** A Team-Building Activity, by
              John E. Jones and Anthony J. Reilly (Time required:
              approximately two hours.)

- To increase team members' understanding of the
  concept of group effectiveness.

- To generate commitment within an intact group to identify its interaction dynamics.

(VIII-131)   **316. Group Sociogram:** Intragroup Communication, by Thomas J. Mallinson, Alan Tolliday, and Ron Sept (Time required: approximately one and one-half hours.)

- To identify existing patterns of interaction and influence in an intact group.

- To increase awareness of the effects of group dynamics on intragroup communication patterns.

(IX-28)   **345. Constructive Criticism:** Rating Leadership Abilities, by Fred E. Woodall (Time required: one and one-half to two hours.)

- To provide an opportunity for the members of an intact group to give and receive feedback regarding their leadership abilities.

- To give the members experience in evaluating themselves and others in a constructive, concrete manner.

(IX-110)   **356. Messages:** A Group Feedback Experience, by Gilles L. Talbot (Time required: approximately forty-five minutes.)

- To examine the thought process, verbal behavior, and risk factor involved in sending verbal messages about feelings.

- To analyze the ways in which the process of sending and receiving such messages contributes to group cohesiveness.

('85-87)   **386. Sharing and Supporting Goals:** A Team-Building Activity, by Richard L. Bunning (Time required: one hour, forty-five minutes to four hours, fifteen minutes.)

- To enhance the team-building process through self-disclosure, feedback, and interpersonal commitment.

- To offer the team members an opportunity to give and receive feedback about work-related, personal-growth goals.

- To develop the team members' commitment to support one another's growth goals.

('85-95)   **388. Smackers:** Group Mid-Life Assessment, by Richard L. Hughes (Time required: approximately two hours.)

- To provide a mid-life assessment and growth experience for an intact group.

- To help the participants to identify behaviors and personal qualities that are valuable within a group.

- To allow the participants to give and receive feedback about the ways in which their behavior and personal qualities are perceived within the group.

- To develop the participants' ability and willingness to evaluate one anothers' behavior and personal qualities in the interest of improving group functioning.

(X-88)   **402. Power and Affection Exchange:** Sharing Feelings, by Gustave J. Rath (Time required: approximately two hours.)

- To offer the participants an opportunity to express their feelings for one another.

- To explore the participants' feelings about power and affection.

(X-92)   **403. Yearbook:** Positive Group Feedback, by Bunty Ketcham and Alan Gilburg (Time required: one hour and forty minutes to two hours.)

- To allow the members of an ongoing group to give and receive positive feedback about their perceived roles within the group.

- To enhance the members' appreciation of themselves and one another.

- To help the members to determine ways in which group functioning might be improved in the future.

('86-41)   **418. Group Sociogram II:** Perceptions of Interaction, by Arlette C. Ballew (Time required: approximately two and one-half hours.)

- To help the members of an intact group to express their perceptions of and feelings about the relationships within the group.

- To identify existing patterns of interaction within an intact group.

- To encourage communication and the sharing of perceptions within the group.

- To "open up" an intact group for team-building efforts.

('88-69)   **444. The Advertising Firm:** A Group Feedback Activity, by Jeanne Lindholm (Time required: approximately one and one-half hours.)

- To develop the participants' awareness of how they work together while completing a task.

- To assist the participants in generating ways to improve their effectiveness as a group.

- To monitor the effect of periodic feedback on an intact group as it completes a task.

- To enhance the participants' understanding of the role of feedback in enhancing a group's effectiveness.

('88-73)   **445. Images:** Envisioning the Ideal Group, by Joseph E. Garcia and Ken S. Keleman (Time required: two to two and one-half hours.)

- To provide an opportunity for the members of an intact group to receive feedback from one another about the perceived image of the group.

- To enable the members to examine the behaviors that lead to particular images of a group.

- To assist the members in developing images by which they would like their group to be known.

- To help the members to develop ways of actualizing these images.

('89-67)   **456. It's in the Cards:** Sharing Team Perceptions, by Frederick A. Miller, Judith H. Katz, and Ava Albert Schnidman (Time required: approximately three hours, depending on the size of the group.)

- To help the participants to clarify how they perceive (1) themselves as team members, (2) their fellow team members, (3) the team as a whole, and (4) the team's relationship to the organization.

- To offer the participants an opportunity to share their perceptions and to provide one another with feedback.

- To assist the participants in working the issues surfaced during the activity.

('90-67)   **468. The Genie's Wish:** Identifying and Addressing Group Needs, by Thomas F. Penderghast (Time required: a minimum of two hours and fifteen minutes based on a five-member group. A period of ten minutes extra is required for each additional member over five.)

- To offer the participants an opportunity to identify what they need, both individually and as a group, in order to work effectively and to learn ways in which those needs might be met.

- To surface important group issues and to encourage group growth.

- To foster the participants' problem-solving skills.

- To offer the participants an opportunity to practice visualizing (as a part of the guided-imagery process).

- To help the participants understand their individual task approaches and how the combination of these different approaches can enhance the group problem-solving process.

('91-43)   **477. Bases of Power:** Developing the Group's Potential, by Mary Harper Kitzmiller and Carol Nolde (Time required: approximately three to three and one-half hours for a group with six members. A group with more than six members may require considerably more time.)

- To acquaint the participants with the different bases of power.

- To assist the participants in identifying the power bases resident in their groups and how those forms of power affect the group.

- To assist the participants in recognizing their own potential for developing and using power.

■ To assist each participant in creating an action plan for enhancing his or her power bases.

('92-47)   **489. Group Calendar:** Celebrating Significant Events, by Marc B. Sokol and Douglas A. Cohen (Time required: one hour to one hour and fifteen minutes.)

■ To offer the participants a nonthreatening method of getting to know one another better.

■ To give the participants the opportunity to remember significant work-related events that took place during the past year and to recognize and appreciate one another's achievements.

■ To allow the participants to compare memories of significant work-related events.

('92-51)   **490. Strengths and Needs:** Using Feedback for Group Development, by Terry Burchett (Time required: This activity is conducted in two sessions. Session 1, sharing feedback, requires two to three and one-half hours, depending on the size of the work group. Session 2, action planning based on the information shared in the first session, requires approximately three hours.)

■ To provide an opportunity for the participants to give one another feedback about the strengths they bring to their work group.

■ To offer the participants a chance to identify what they like on the job and what they would like to change and then to share this information with one another.

■ To provide a structure through which the participants can express what they need from one another.

- To provide an opportunity for the participants to do action planning based on their strengths, likes, items they would like to change, and needs.

TEAMS: Conflict and Intergroup Issues

Conflict

(X-106)   **406. Ajax Appliance Corporation:** Exploring Conflict-Management Styles, by Judith L. Grewell, Michael L. Gracey, Geraldine Platt, and Dale N. DeHaven (Time required: two hours and twenty minutes.)

- To illustrate various approaches to managing conflict and the ways in which these approaches affect the process of resolving a problem.

- To offer the participants opportunities to practice assigned approaches and to experiment with alternative approaches during role plays involving conflict.

(X-126)   **409. Sharing Perspectives:** Exchanging Views on Managerial and Worker Attitudes (Time required: approximately two hours.)

- To explore the origins of certain managerial and worker attitudes.

- To allow the participants to share and discuss their personal feelings about these attitudes.

- To help a manager and his or her subordinates to develop a greater understanding of one another so that their relationships can be improved in the future.

('91-119)   **483. Conflict Management:** Developing a Procedure, by Larry Porter (Time required: one hour and forty minutes to two hours and fifteen minutes.)

■ To acquaint the members of an intact work group with some guidelines for resolving a conflict with another person by giving useful feedback.

■ To help the group members to develop their own procedure for managing conflict.

Intergroup Issues

(II-62)   **036. Win As Much As You Can:** An Intergroup Competition, based on W. Gellermann (Time required: approximately one hour.)

■ To dramatize the merits of both competitive and collaborative models within the context of intragroup and intergroup relations.

■ To illustrate the impact of win-lose situations.

(III-81)   **068. Intergroup Meeting:** An Image Exchange (Time required: three hours.)

■ To improve the relationship between two groups, such as levels of management, majority-minority groups, males and females.

■ To explore how groups interact with each other.

('72-36)   **081. Intergroup Model Building:** The LEGO® Man, by W.B. Reddy and Otto Kroeger (Time required: approximately two hours.)

- To extract the learnings from a competitive teamwork experience, in terms of leadership style, developing alternatives, dominance and submission within teams, and distribution of work and resources.

- To diagnose the dynamics of an intact group in terms of role taking.

('75-51)   **145. Win What, Lose What?:** An Intergroup Conflict Intervention, by Kenneth Finn (Time required: approximately three hours.)

- To examine the elements of intergroup conflict.

- To illustrate the process of conflict resolution.

(V-5)   **150. Riddles:** Intergroup Competition, by Brian P. Holleran (Time required: approximately one and one-half hours.)

- To observe competitive behavior among groups.

- To determine how a group interacts with other groups when it is dependent on them for the completion of its task.

('81-48)   **289. Intergroup Clearing:** A Relationship-Building Intervention, by Lawrence C. Porter (Time required: approximately three hours.)

- To "clear the air" between two work groups (departments, divisions, units, teams).

- To develop intergroup understanding and acceptance.

- To create the basis for an improved relationship between groups.

(X-118)   **407. The Value Profile:** Legitimizing Intergroup Differences, by Edward F. Pajak (Time required: one hour and forty-five minutes to two hours.)

- To help two work groups within an organization to understand and accept the legitimacy of each other's values so that they can interact more effectively.

- To assist each group in establishing its own profile of values.

CONSULTING AND FACILITATING:
Consulting: Awareness

('73-32)   **098. Strategies of Changing:** A Multiple-Role-Play, by David Marion and Ann Edelman (Time required: approximately one hour.)

- To acquaint people with three different interpersonal strategies for trying to effect change in human systems.

(IV-34)   **110. Organization Structures:** Communication Patterns, by Tom Irwin (Time required: approximately one hour.)

- To demonstrate the varying effectiveness of different organization structures.

- To diagnose working relationships within an intact group.

- To illustrate less efficient modes of communication.

- To illustrate perceived alienation.

(V-85)　　**163. Coloring Book:** An Organization Experiment, based on Michael J. Miller (Time required: approximately one and one-half hours.)

- To explore relationships between organizational design and task complexity.

(V-98)　　**165. Marbles:** A Community Experiment, adapted from Frederick L. Goodman (Time required: approximately two hours.)

- To study community from the perspectives of establishing, enforcing, and interpreting rules.

- To explore rule-governed behaviors.

('77-22)　　**188. Tug O' War:** A Force-Field Psychodrama, by Gerhard Friedrich (Time required: approximately one hour; one-half hour minimum; repetition with additional problems could take two hours.)

- To demonstrate the dynamics in a force-field analysis of a change situation.

- To involve participants in a problem-solving process.

('78-71)　　**232. MANDOERS:** Organizational Clarification, by Thomas H. Patten, Jr. (Time required: two to two and one-half hours.)

- To enable groups undergoing team-building efforts within the same organization to examine management and employee development, organizational effectiveness, and reward systems in the work organization.

- To explore the diversity of views among participants regarding complex social and behavioral phenomena.

- To examine feelings resulting from organizational problems and to identify corrective actions that can be taken to deal with them.

('83-77)   **339. Organizational Blasphemies:** Clarifying Values, by Tony McNulty (Time required: one to one and one-half hours.)

- To provide an opportunity for the participants to be creatively open about aspects of their organizations.

- To identify and compare the organizational values of the group members.

- To provide an opportunity to explore the match between the goals or values of the participants and those of the organization.

(IX-136)   **360. Matrix:** Balancing Organizational Needs, by James P. Lewis (Time required: approximately two hours.)

- To allow the participants to become acquainted with and experience a matrix organizational structure.

- To demonstrate the rewards and difficulties experienced by a group that concentrates on task and process simultaneously.

('84-55)   **372. The Shoe-Distribution Company:** Exploring the Impact of Organizational Roles, by Marc A. Silverman (Time required: approximately two and one-half hours.)

- To explore organizational dynamics.

- To help the participants to identify motivating forces within different organizational roles.

■ To provide an opportunity for the participants to observe competition and/or collaboration as a result of organizational dynamics and roles.

(X-132)   **410. The People of Trion:** Exploring Organizational Values, by B.J. Allen, Jr. (Time required: approximately two hours.)

■ To offer the participants an opportunity to examine their organizational values.

■ To explore the implications of the participants' organizational values.

■ To explore the implications of differences between personal and organizational values.

■ To examine the ways in which people are taught organizational values.

('88-77)   **446. Dos and Don'ts:** Developing Guidelines for Change, by Homer H. Johnson (Time required: approximately two hours.)

■ To enable the participants to identify their reactions to change in organizations.

■ To assist the participants in developing guidelines for suggesting and implementing change in organizations.

('91-65)   **479. Prairie General Hospital:** Parallel Learning Structures, by Abraham B. Shani and Daniel M. Wise (Time required: two and one-half hours.)

■ To help participants to recognize bureaucratic barriers to problem solving within an organization.

- To demonstrate the use of parallel learning structure interventions toward more optimal utilization of human resources.

- To help participants to develop methods for cross-boundary organizational dialog mechanisms within bureaucratic structures.

('93-75)   **505. The Hundredth Monkey:** Sharing Mind-Sets, by Marian K. Prokop (Time required: approximately two hours.)

- To introduce participants to the concept of shared mind-set.

- To offer participants the opportunity to explore four types of shared mind-set.

- To offer participants the opportunity to explore options for promoting a shared organizational mind-set.

('94-93)   **517. Hats "R" Us:** Learning About Organizational Cultures, by Catherine J. Nagy (Time required: approximately two hours and thirty to forty-five minutes.)

- To introduce the participants to four general types of organizational culture.

- To provide the participants with an opportunity to identify the culture of their own organization.

- To offer the participants an opportunity to explore their personal alignment or misalignment with their organization's culture.

CONSULTING AND FACILITATING:
Consulting: Diagnosing/Skills

('74-24)   **131. Roxboro Electric Company:** An OD Role-Play, by Harvey Thomson with B. Bell, M. Brosseau, P. Fleck, and E. Kahn (Time required: approximately two and one-half hours.)

- To provide an experience in sensing organizational problems.

- To provide feedback on interviewing effectiveness.

- To explore organizational diagnosis and action planning.

('76-53)   **183. Consulting Triads:** Self-Assessment, by Anthony G. Banet, Jr. (Time required: approximately two hours.)

- To assess consultation skills.

- To provide practice in one-to-one consultation.

('77-39)   **193. Tri-State:** A Multiple Role Play, by Hank Karp (Time required: approximately two and one-half hours.)

- To build skills in diagnosing organizational and group problems.

- To focus attention on the interrelationship between content and process issues.

(VI-66)   **211. HELPCO:** An OD Role Play, by Neil E. Rand (Time required: approximately three hours.)

- To study the processes of organization development (OD) consultation.

- To develop OD diagnosis, consultation, and observation skills.

- To compare the relative effectiveness of two or more forms of group leadership in competing work teams.

('78-55)   **230. Willington:** An Intervention-Skills Role Play, by W. Alan Randolph, John C. Ferrie, and David D. Palmer (Time required: two and one-half to three hours.)

- To determine the appropriate intervention strategy for a simulated organization.

- To implement a strategy for entering, initially diagnosing, and contracting with the simulated organization.

- To provide feedback on the consulting team members' interventions skills and strategy.

- To explore theory, skills, values, and strategies of organization development (OD).

(IX-34)   **347. Elm Street Community Church:** Third-Party Consultation, by Charles E. List (Time required: approximately three hours.)

- To provide the participants with an experience that simulates collaborative problem solving within an organization.

- To develop the participants' understanding of the role of a process consultant.

- To build skills in diagnosing organizational and group problems.

(IX-48)　　**348. Inquiries:** Observing and Building Hypotheses, by Steven E. Aufrecht (Time required: approximately two hours.)

- To provide the participants with experience in discovering relationships and meanings in an unfamiliar situation.

- To help the participants to become aware of their own methods of observing, gathering data, and building hypotheses.

- To allow the participants an opportunity to test the validity of these methods.

('85-81)　　**385. Measuring Excellence:** Applying the Lessons of Peters and Waterman, by Leonard D. Goodstein (Time required: approximately three and one-half hours.)

- To help managers within an organization to identify their organization's degree of excellence.

- To develop a sense of cohesiveness and teamwork within management groups.

- To heighten the participants' awareness of existing management attitudes and practices within their organization.

- To enhance the participants' commitment to organizational excellence.

(X-148)　　**412. Client Concerns:** Developing Appropriate Trainer Responses (Time required: one hour and forty-five minutes.)

- To develop the participants' skills in devising appropriate responses to representative client statements.

- To offer the participants an opportunity to explore ways of handling various client concerns and expectations.

- To help the participants to identify their individual biases about various training issues.

('86-79)   **424. The Client-Consultant Questionnaire:** Checking for Client Involvement in OD, by Arlette C. Ballew (Time required: one and one-half to two hours.)

- To present a way of determining whether a client really is involved in or committed to an organization development effort.

- To acquaint the participants with potential differences in diagnoses, values, and needs between a consultant and a client.

- To explore the potential for collusion for power and influence between the client and the consultant.

('89-101)   **460. City of Buffington:** Developing Consultation Skills, by Willa M. Bruce (Time required: approximately two hours and fifteen to thirty minutes.)

- To provide the participants with an experience in diagnosing organizational problems.

- To offer the participants an opportunity to practice interviewing for the purpose of obtaining information for diagnosing organizational problems.

- To allow the participants to practice giving and receiving feedback on consulting skills used during data-gathering interviews.

('91-125)   **484. Metaphors:** Characterizing the Organization, by J. William Pfeiffer (Time required: two hours to two hours and fifteen minutes.)

- To offer the participants a way to clarify and discuss their perceptions of their organization.

- To allow the participants to compare their perceptions of an ideal organization with their perceptions of their own organization.

- To provide the participants with a means for analyzing their organization as they perceive it and for determining specific organizational changes that they would like to make.

('92-79)   **493. Working at Our Company:** Clarifying Organizational Values, by Leonard D. Goodstein (Time required: approximately two hours.)

- To offer the participants an opportunity to examine and to discuss their personal and organizational values.

- To encourage the participants to explore the interaction of personal and organizational values.

- To enhance the participants' effectiveness as team members.

('92-87)   **494. Help Wanted:** Collaborative Problem Solving for Consultants, by Carol Nolde (Time required: approximately two and one-half hours.)

- To offer the participants an opportunity to practice collaborative problem solving in one-on-one consulting situations and to receive feedback on their efforts.

- To assist the participants in identifying which consultant behaviors are effective in collaborative problem solving and which are not effective.

('93-85)   **506. International Equity Claims Department:** Designing Work, by Homer H. Johnson and Karen S. Tschanz (Time required: approximately two to three hours.)

- To introduce the participants to the basic elements of work design and the application of these elements.

- To explore the value of work design that takes into account the needs of those who do the work as well as the needs of the customer and what needs to be done.

- To encourage the participants to focus on a work process that is driven by customer and employee needs, a vision for the work design, and measurable work-process goals.

CONSULTING AND FACILITATING:
Facilitating: Opening

(I-3)   **001. Listening and Inferring:** A Getting-Acquainted Activity (Time required: fifteen minutes.)

- To facilitate the involvement of individuals in a newly formed group.

(I-5)   **002. Two-Four-Eight:** Building Teams (Time required: approximately thirty minutes.)

- To divide a large group into workable subgroups in such a way as to increase group cohesiveness and identity.

(I-19)　**005. Who Am I?:** A Getting-Acquainted Activity (Time required: approximately forty-five minutes.)

- To allow participants to become acquainted quickly in a relatively nonthreatening way.

(II-3)　**025. Group Conversation:** Discussion Starters, by Dave Castle (Time required: can be a fifteen-minute preface to other group activities or planned for an entire meeting.)

- To develop a compatible climate and readiness for interaction in a group through sharing personal experience.

(II-10)　**027. Jigsaw:** Forming Groups (Time required: approximately thirty minutes.)

- To establish group cohesion by forming a large number of participants into groups with pre-determined compositions.

(II-88)　**042. First Names, First Impressions:** A Feedback Experience, by John E. Jones (Time required: approximately one hour.)

- To get acquainted with other members of a small group.

- To discover one's initial impact on others.

- To study phenomena related to first impressions—their accuracy and effects.

(III-3)　**049. "Who Am I?" Variations:** A Getting-Acquainted Activity (Time required: approximately forty-five minutes.)

- To allow participants to become acquainted quickly in a relatively nonthreatening way.

('73-9)   **088. "Cold" Introductions:** Getting Acquainted, by John E. Jones (Time required: approximately three minutes per participant.)

- To help participants to get to know each other while building expectations of risk taking and receptivity to feedback.

- To build norms of openness, experimentation, and attention to process.

(IV-3)   **101. Getting Acquainted:** A Potpourri (Time required: varies with each listed experience.)

- To be used as ice breakers in human relations training events.

('74-7)   **125. Hum-Dinger:** A Getting-Acquainted Activity, by A. Donald Duncan (Time required: approximately thirty minutes.)

- To break a large group into smaller groups in a nonthreatening manner.

- To facilitate contact between all members of a large group in a related climate of fun and humor.

- To explore a novel way of generating movement and activity.

(V-3)   **149. Energizers:** Group Starters (Time required: varies with each activity.)

- To prepare participants for meetings.

('76-7)   **173. Limericks:** Getting Acquainted, by Elizabeth Racicot (Time required: approximately thirty minutes.)

- To acquaint and involve participants with one another through nonthreatening physical activity.

- To divide a large group into subgroups in a climate of humor and cohesiveness.

('76-10)   **174. Labeling:** A Getting-Acquainted Activity, by Charles L. Kormanski (Time required: approximately one hour.)

- To provide opportunities to become acquainted with other members of a group.

- To promote feedback and self-disclosure among participants regarding initial perceptions.

(VI-3)   **197. Best Friend:** A Getting-Acquainted Activity, by Donald L. Garris (Time required: approximately forty-five minutes.)

- To afford participants the opportunity to introduce themselves in a nonthreatening manner.

- To develop a climate for group interaction by sharing personal information.

(VI-7)   **198. Choose an Object:** A Getting-Acquainted Activity, by Donald L. Thompson (Time required: approximately two hours.)

- To increase perception of oneself.

- To provide an opportunity to share personal perceptions.

- To provide an opportunity to receive feedback on perceived behavior.

(VII-5)   **245. Tea Party:** An Ice Breaker, by Don Keyworth (Time required: fifteen minutes to one hour.)

- To allow participants to share experiences and perceptions in a nonthreatening manner.

- To promote acquaintance and a feeling of interaction in a new group.

('80-11)   **269. Autographs:** An Ice Breaker, by John E. Jones (Time required: approximately one-half hour.)

- To facilitate the getting-acquainted process in a large group.

- To alleviate anxiety experienced during the beginning of a training session.

('81-9)   **281. Alliterative Names:** A Getting-Acquainted Activity (Time required: approximately one-half hour.)

- To facilitate the getting-acquainted process in a large group.

- To promote self-disclosure in a new group.

('81-11)   **282. Birth Signs:** An Ice Breaker, by John E. Jones (Time required: approximately one-half hour.)

- To facilitate the getting-acquainted process in a large group.

- To alleviate the participants' anxiety at the beginning of a training session.

(VIII-5)   **293. Name Tags:** An Ice Breaker, by Don Martin and Cynthia Cherrey (Time required: fifteen minutes.)

- To provide participants with an opportunity to introduce themselves in a nonthreatening and enjoyable manner.

- To develop an atmosphere conducive to group interaction.

(VIII-7)   **294. Learning Exchange:** A Getting-Acquainted Activity, by Andy F. Farquharson (Time required: approximately one hour.)

- To provide an opportunity for participants to get to know each other.

- To demonstrate the knowledge and skills that the participants have brought to the group.

- To raise awareness of factors that enhance the teaching-learning process.

('82-9)   **317. Rebus Names:** Getting Acquainted, by Anne Davis Toppins (Time required: one hour.)

- To facilitate the getting-acquainted process among members of a new group.

- To facilitate the involvement and interaction of individuals in a newly formed group.

('83-11)   **329. Just the Facts:** Getting Acquainted, by Robert N. Glenn (Time required: one to one and one-half hours.)

- To provide an opportunity for members of a group to become acquainted with one another in a nonthreatening manner.

- To create an atmosphere conducive to group interaction and sharing.

(IX-8)   **342. News Bulletin:** Focusing the Group, by Fred E. Woodall (Time required: approximately five minutes per member.)

- To develop readiness for interaction at the beginning of a group session.

- To free group members from personal concerns so that they can concentrate on group matters.

('84-92)   **376. Group Savings Bank:** An Introductory Experience, by Debera Libkind and Dennis M. Dennis (Time required: approximately forty-five minutes.)

- To help the participants to become acquainted with one another.

- To develop the participants' readiness for involvement at the beginning of a group session.

- To provide the participants with an opportunity to experiment with abandoning old behaviors and/or adopting new behaviors.

('85-91)   **387. Daffodil:** Getting Acquainted in Small Groups, by Michael D. Laus (Time required: approximately forty-five minutes.)

- To assemble the participants into small groups in a nonthreatening manner.

- To facilitate the getting-acquainted process by generating contact among the participants.

('86-11)   **413. Getting To Know You:** Different Approaches, Different Perceptions, by David E. Whiteside (Time required: one to one and one-half hours; larger groups will require more time.)

- To introduce group members to one another.

- To demonstrate that our perceptions of others and our interactions with them are influenced by the information we solicit from them.

('87-87)   **436. I Represent:** A World Meeting, by Patrick Doyle (Time required: one to one and one-half hours.)

- To facilitate the getting-acquainted process.

- To enable participants to express indirectly how they would like to be perceived.

('93-93)   **507. Color Me:** Getting Acquainted, by Jacque Chapman (Time required: approximately forty-five minutes with twenty participants.)

- To introduce the participants to one another.

- To offer the participants an opportunity to become acquainted in a way that allows them to reveal as much or as little about themselves as they wish.

('94-107)   **518. Parsley, Garlic, Ginger, Pepper:** Introductions, by Marian K. Prokop (Time required: forty-five minutes to one hour.)

- To introduce the participants to one another.

- To develop an atmosphere conducive to group interaction.

CONSULTING AND FACILITATING:
Facilitating: Blocks to Learning

('73-11)   **089. Gunnysack:** An Introduction to Here-and-Now, by John E. Jones (Time required: approximately thirty minutes.)

- To establish the norm of attending to here-and-now data and "gunnysacking" then-and-there data.

- To help participants to become aware of their own here-and-now reactions.

('73-15)   **091. Perception of Task:** A Teaching-Learning Exercise, by Robert T. Williams (Time required: one hour.)

- To examine how perceptions of a learning task by teacher and learner influence teaching styles and learning styles.

(IV-41)   **112. The "T" Test:** An Experiential Lecture on Traits, by Anthony J. Reilly (Time required: approximately thirty minutes.)

- To introduce the concept of personality traits.

- To illustrate the process of inferring characteristics from behavior.

- To help diminish some of the unproductive anxiety which is often associated with filling out psychological instruments on inventories.

('77-32)   **191. Communication Analysis:** A Getting-Acquainted Activity, by Ronald D. Jorgenson (Time required: approximately one hour.)

- To establish a laboratory-learning climate in the initial stages of a group composed of hostile or reluctant participants.

- To experience openness in exploring positive and negative feelings in a nonthreatening atmosphere.

- To examine how affective elements, especially negative feelings, influence the result of communication.

('79-13)   **234. Buttermilk:** Awareness Expansion, by Thomas R. Harvey (Time required: one-half hour.)

- To demonstrate the processes of interpersonal influence and personal change.

- To "warm up" groups that are interested in exploring the dynamics of change.

(VIII-37)   **301. Resistance to Learning:** Developing New Skills, by Hyler Bracey and Roy Trueblood (Time required: two hours.)

- To provide a model for understanding the phenomenon of behavioral resistance in learning situations.

- To demonstrate various behavioral manifestations of resistance.

- To increase awareness of techniques that can be used to overcome resistance in learning situations.

('82-46)   **324. Needs, Expectations, and Resources:** Beginning a Workshop, by Joel Goodman and James A. Bellanca (Time required: one and one-half to two hours.)

- To allow participants in a long-term training workshop to become acquainted with one another.

- To identify and clarify the needs, expectations, and resources of the group facilitator and the participants in a long-term training workshop.

- To establish a cooperative, nonthreatening climate in the workshop group.

CONSULTING AND FACILITATING:
Facilitating: Skills

(I-75)   **016. Fantasies:** Suggestions for Individuals and Groups (Time required: varies.)

■ To promote heightened awareness of self and others.

(I-86)   **019. Awareness Expansion:** A Potpourri (Time required: varies.)

■ To heighten one's sensory awareness.

(I-107)   **024. Assumptions about Human Relations Training:** An Opinionnaire, by John E. Jones, Jim Dickinson, Carla Dee, and B. Howard Arbes (Time required: minimum of one hour.)

■ To allow the group to assess the degree to which it has consensus on a number of assumptions that underlie laboratory learning.

■ To assist co-facilitators in identifying each other's biases about training.

■ To discover some possible "blind spots" that the training staff may have about training.

(II-7)   **026. Miniversity:** Sharing Participants' Ideas (Time required: time is dependent on the size of the group, the facilities available, and the number of "courses" offered.)

■ To provide for dissemination of information, using participants as resources, during a conference, workshop, or institute.

(II-91)   **043. Verbal Activities Within Groups:** A Potpourri (Time required: varies with each activity.)

- To be used as openers when meetings of the groups are infrequent, or may be used as interventions within meetings.

(II-94)   **044. Nonverbal Communication:** A Collection (Time required: varies with each activity.)

- To learn new ways of expressing one's feelings, independent of one's vocabulary.

- To express feelings authentically using nonverbal symbolism.

- To focus on nonverbal cues that one emits.

(II-97)   **045. Helping Pairs:** A Collection (Time required: varies with each activity.)

- To build helping relationships ancillary to small-group experiences.

- To give participants an opportunity to try out new behavior within a dyadic relationship.

- To provide group members with ways of checking out their perceptions of and reactions to laboratory experiences.

(II-113)   **047. Microlab:** A Training Demonstration (Time required: depends on variations employed in the design.)

- To demonstrate human relations training methods

- To accelerate the development of growth-producing norms, such as openness and attention to feelings.

(II-115)   **048. Process Intervention:** A Facilitator Practice Session
(Time required: at least one hour.)

- To provide practice in intervening in small groups.

- To generate feedback on intervention styles.

(III-8)   **051. Empty Chair:** An Extended Group Design (Time
required: open.)

- To allow all participants to become involved voluntarily
  in a group-on-group experience when the size of the
  total group makes discussion impractical.

(III-97)   **072. Nonverbal Communication:** A Collection (Time
required: varies with each activity.)

- To learn new ways of expressing one's feelings,
  independent of one's vocabulary.

- To express feelings authentically using nonverbal
  symbolism.

- To focus on nonverbal cues that one emits.

('73-17)   **092. Medial Feedback:** A "Mid-Course Correction"
Exercise (Time required: approximately one and one-half
hours.)

- To generate evaluative data about the effects of a
  laboratory education design while there is still time to
  modify it.

- To study group process phenomena both as a
  participant and as an observer.

('73-29)   **096. Participant-Staff Expectations:** Reducing the Gap, by
Adolfo H. Munoz (Time required: approximately one
hour.)

- To provide participants and facilitators the opportunity to examine and discuss mutual expectations and perceptions regarding the training program.

- To reduce the "expectation gap" between participants and facilitators.

('75-63)   **148. Group Leadership Functions:** A Facilitator-Style Activity, by Robert K. Conyne (Time required: approximately two hours.)

- To explore four basic leadership functions of group facilitators.

- To study the relationship between leadership functions and general interpersonal style.

(IX-159)   **363. Training Philosophies:** A Personal Assessment, by G.E.H. Beamish (Time required: one hour.)

- To assist the participants in clarifying their individual training philosophies.

- To help the participants to clarify their perceptions of the relationship between training and management.

('92-97)   **495. Good Workshops Don't Just Happen:** Developing Facilitation Skills, by Kathleen Kreis (Time required: approximately two hours.)

- To assist the participants in identifying elements of facilitation that are (1) vital to workshop effectiveness, (2) harmful to workshop effectiveness, and (3) reflective of style (rather than vital or harmful).

- To offer the participants an opportunity to consider and discuss facilitation practices, techniques, and styles.

('92-11)   **496. Up Close and Personal with Dr. Maslow:** Designing Training to Meet Trainees' Needs, by Bonnie Jameson (Time required: approximately three hours.)

■ To explore Abraham Maslow's (1970) theory of the hierarchy of needs as the basis for creating a positive learning climate in a training experience.

■ To present a format for designing a training module.

■ To offer the participants an opportunity to practice designing and presenting a training module that meets trainees' needs.

('93-97)   **508. Zodiac for Trainers:** Determining Competencies, by Bonnie Jameson (Time required: one hour and forty minutes to two hours.)

■ To assist the participants in identifying attitudes and skills that they feel are essential to being an effective human resources development (HRD) trainer.

■ To provide the participants with an opportunity to assess their levels of competence in various trainer attitudes and skills.

■ To offer the participants an opportunity to discuss ways to capitalize on their strengths as trainers and ways to address their areas for improvement as trainers.

('94-115)   **519. Disability Awareness:** Providing Equal Opportunities in the Training Environment, by Robert William (Bob) Lucas (Time required: one hour and fifteen minutes to one hour and thirty minutes. Additional time is required to prepare the room for the activity [see Physical Setting].)

- To raise the participants' awareness of the need to provide equal access to training opportunities for persons with disabilities.

- To allow the participants to experience the potential frustrations that persons with disabilities may encounter in an environment or activity that does not accommodate them.

- To provide a model activity for use in disability-awareness training.

CONSULTING AND FACILITATING:
Facilitating: Closing

('72-61)   **086. Symbolic Closing Exercise,** by Maury Smith (Time required: approximately ten minutes.)

- To finish a workshop or laboratory with a sense of closure.

- To re-enact the group process in symbolic nonverbal action.

(IV-49)   **114. Closure:** Variations on a Theme (Time required: varies with each idea.)

- To be useful in closing human relations training events.

- Can also be employed to foster self-disclosure in personal growth groups.

('75-54)   **146. Payday:** A Closure Activity, by Richard L. Bunning (Time required: approximately one hour.)

- To provide for self- and group evaluation of each participant's performance within the group.

- To allow each participant to compare his or her self-evaluation with the group's evaluation.

- To give participants experience in evaluating others in a constructive, concrete manner.

('76-17)   **176. Symbolic Toast:** A Closure Experience, by A. Donald Duncan and Jo F. Dorris (Time required: approximately forty minutes.)

- To provide closure at the end of a training experience.

- To provide an opportunity for participants to give and receive feedback.

- To allow each person to receive some personal validation from each member of the group.

- To affirm the personal strengths of the participants.

(VI-19)   **201. Bread Making:** An Integrating Experience, by Anthony G. Banet, Jr. (Time required: approximately one hour and twenty minutes. [one sixty-minute period followed by one twenty-minute period later on].)

- To experience collaborating on an unusual group task.

- To focus on the sensory, fantasy, and creative aspects of food preparation.

- To provide a sensory, nonverbal background for integrating learning in the final stages of a workshop.

('78-12)   **222. Golden Awards:** A Closure Activity, by John Elliott-Kemp and Graham Williams (Time required: approximately two hours.)

- To provide an opportunity for group and self-appraisal.

- To allow members a chance to see how others perceive them.

- To practice giving feedback to others in a constructive and helpful manner.

('82-12) **318. Kia Ora:** Closure, by Peter M. Swain (Time required: approximately thirty to forty-five minutes.)

- To provide closure at the end of a training experience.

- To provide an opportunity for participants to express feelings generated by the group experience.

- To introduce the aspects of Maori culture that pertain to interpersonal encounter.

(X-5) **389. Aloha:** A Feedback Activity, by Thomas H. Patten, Jr. (Time required: approximately forty-five minutes.)

- To offer the participants an opportunity to give and receive feedback about their strengths and opportunities for improvement in interpersonal relations.

- To provide closure at the end of an experiential-learning event.

LEADERSHIP: Ethics

('75-7) **137. What Do You See?:** A Discovery Activity, by Arthur G. Kirn (Time required: a minimum of one hour.)

- To expand awareness of these things that have meaning for life and work.

- To discover new areas of individual relevance and interest.

- To promote changing negative thinking to positive thinking.

('75-43)   **143. Ideal Cards:** A Self-Disclosure Activity, by Brian P. Holleran (Time required: approximately one and one-half hours.)

- To encourage interaction and self-disclosure about ideals.

- To reveal group members' priorities for their ideals.

('79-15)   **235. Who Killed John Doe?:** A Value-Clarification Activity, by Charles A. Hart (Time required: approximately one hour.)

- To articulate individual opinions about social and individual responsibilities.

- To explore and clarify personal values.

- To participate in shared decision making.

(VII-11)   **246. Personal Identity:** An Ice Breaker, by David E. Whiteside (Time required: approximately one hour.)

- To enable participants to "try on" new identities.

- To explore the influence of a different identity on the behavior of others.

- To explore the relationship between honesty and trust.

('81-13)   **283. Louisa's Problem:** Value Clarification, by Cassandra E. Amesley (Time required: approximately two hours.)

- To provide practice in clarifying issues and identifying values without passing judgment.

- To develop awareness of some of the factors affecting one's own value judgments and those of others.

- To provide an opportunity to exchange various points of view on a highly emotional issue.

(IX-146) **361. Values and Decisions:** Checking for Congruence, by Gib Akin (Time required: one hour and forty-five minutes.)

- To help the participants to clarify their personal values.

- To explore the relationship between the participants' values and their major life decisions.

- To identify factors that affect commitment to values in decision making.

(X-142) **411. The Gold Watch:** Balancing Personal and Professional Values, by Michael R. Lavery (Time required: two hours.)

- To provide an opportunity for the participants to examine, identify, and clarify their personal and professional values.

- To allow the participants to explore the interrelationship of personal values and values expressed by and in organizations.

LEADERSHIP: Interviewing/Appraisal

('75-40) **142. Live Case:** A Group Diagnosis, by Robert K. Conyne and David H. Frey (Time required: approximately two hours.)

- To illustrate problems involved in overgeneralizing.

- To practice interviewing techniques as a method of generating data about an individual.

- To study the process of forming hypotheses from available information.

(VII-73)   **257. Sunglow:** An Appraisal Role Play, by J. Malcolm Rigby (Time required: two to two and one-half hours.)

- To practice skills in counseling, coaching, and active listening.

- To increase awareness of behavioral and interpersonal factors that influence an interview.

- To provide feedback on interviewing effectiveness.

('83-31)   **333. Assistant Wanted:** An Employment Interview, by Laura M. Graves and Charles A. Lowe (Time required: approximately two to two and one-half hours.)

- To provide participants with an experience in interviewing and in being interviewed.

- To explore the dynamics of the interviewer-interviewee relationship.

- To introduce the components of the employment interview.

(IX-122)   **358. Interviewing:** Gathering Pertinent Information, by Kenneth L. Murrell (Time required: one hour and forty-five minutes.)

- To help the participants to become familiar with the interviewing process from the interviewer's point of view.

- To allow the participants to practice developing criteria that a job candidate must meet based on the nature and duties of the job.

- To assist the participants in developing ways to elicit pertinent information from job candidates.

('84-9) **365. Inquiries and Discoveries:** Managing Interviewing Situations, by Elizabeth Solender (Time required: one and one-half to two hours.)

- To identify effective and ineffective interviewing skills.

- To help the participants to develop skills in conducting interviews with different types of respondents.

('84-49) **371. Constructive Discipline:** Following Organizational Guidelines, by Allen J. Schuh (Time required: approximately two hours.)

- To help the participants to develop an understanding of the importance and complexity of discipline problems within an organization.

- To develop the participants' awareness of the guidelines that can be used to handle discipline problems.

('86-73) **423. BARS:** Developing Behaviorally Anchored Rating Scales, by Dana L. Farrow and John A. Sample (Time required: approximately three hours and forty minutes. Varies depending on the size of the group.)

- To collaboratively construct behaviorally anchored rating scales (BARS) for the relevant dimensions of a specific job position.

- To develop an example of a behaviorally based system of performance measurement.

('87-11)   **425. Performance Appraisal:** A Practice Session, by John E. Oliver (Time required: approximately two and one-half hours.)

- To give participants an opportunity to create agenda for performance appraisals.

- To allow participants to experience the roles of supervisor, subordinate, and observer in a performance appraisal.

- To provide participants with an opportunity to give and receive feedback on performance-appraisal techniques.

('89-23)   **451. What's Legal?:** Investigating Employment-Interview Questions, by Robert J. ("Jack") Cantwell (Time required: approximately two hours and forty-five minutes.)

- To develop the participants' awareness of legal issues in connection with interviewing applicants for employment.

- To assist the participants in identifying legal and illegal employment-interview questions and in determining why they are legal or illegal.

- To give the participants an opportunity to practice devising legal employment-interview questions.

LEADERSHIP: Motivation

('73-43)   **100. Motivation:** A Feedback Exercise, by Donald F. Michalak (Time required: at least one-half hour.)

- To learn the concepts in Maslow's Need Hierarchy.

- To get feedback on one's use of motivational techniques in terms of Maslow's Need Hierarchy.

(VI-28)   **204. Motivation:** A Supervisory-Skill Activity, by Ken Frey and J. David Jackson (Time required: approximately one hour.)

- To demonstrate the value of goal setting for task achievement.

- To demonstrate the positive role of a supervisor in developing the motivation to achieve.

(VI-61)   **210. Darts:** Competition and Motivation, by Samuel Dolinsky (Time required: approximately one and one-half hours.)

- To develop awareness of the factors involved in motivation.

- To increase awareness of the effects of motivation/incentives on the attitudes and performance of a given task in an intergroup competitive situation.

(VII-46)   **253. Penny Pitch:** Demonstrating Reinforcement Styles, by Bradford F. Spencer (Time required: approximately one hour.)

- To demonstrate how positive or negative reinforcement can affect motivation and task accomplishment.

- To increase awareness of responses to interventions made by persons with position and status.

(VIII-10)   **295. People on the Job:** Expressing Opinions, by Martin B. Ross (Time required: one and one-half to two hours.)

- To afford participants the opportunity to share their views in a structured environment.

- To provide a sense of the variety of opinions and attitudes that exist about a particular subject.

- To develop a climate for future group interaction.

(IX-102)   **354. The Manager's Guidebook:** Understanding Motivation, by Kenneth L. Murrell (Time required: approximately two and one-half hours.)

- To provide the participants with a situation in which the issues of motivation can be explored.

- To help the participants to enhance their understanding of the concept of motivation.

('84-22)   **367. MACE:** Demonstrating Factors that Affect Performance, by Stephen Dakin and Russell Robb (Time required: one to one and one-half hours.)

- To demonstrate that individual performance within a group is influenced by four major factors: *motivation, ability, conditions,* and *expectations* (MACE).

('87-45)   **430. There's Never Time To Do It Right:** A Relay Task, by Russell J. Denz (Time required: approximately one hour.)

- To help participants understand the dilemma of quality versus quantity in terms of productivity.

- To help participants explore the consequences of focusing primarily on quality or quantity in teamwork.

('89-39)   **452. Four Factors:** The Influence of Leader Behavior, by William N. Parker (Time required: approximately one hour and forty-five minutes.)

- To acquaint the participants with Rosenthal and Jacobson's (1968) four-factor theory explaining a leader's influence on followers and the effect of this influence on follower behavior.

- To give the participants an opportunity to analyze case studies showing how particular leader approaches to Rosenthal and Jacobson's four factors (climate, feedback, input, and output) can positively or negatively affect followers.

LEADERSHIP: Diversity/Stereotyping

(II-32)   **033. Hollow Square:** A Communications Experiment, by Arthur Shedlin and Warren H. Schmidt (Time required: approximately one hour.)

- To study dynamics involved in planning a task to be carried out by others.

- To study dynamics involved in accomplishing a task planned by others.

- To explore both helpful and hindering communication behaviors in assigning and carrying out a task.

(II-41)   **034. Hampshire In-Basket:** A Management Activity, by J. William Pfeiffer (Time required: approximately three hours.)

- To discover general management principles through personal involvement with problem solving.

- To examine one's management style.

- To plan applications of management principles.

(V-49)   **158. Absentee:** A Management Role Play, by Richard J. Carpenter, Jr. (Time required: approximately one and one-half hours.)

- To explore the dynamics of decision making.

- To study the resolution and management of conflict.

- To reveal loyalty patterns among peers and superiors.

(VIII-52)   **304. When to Delegate:** A Manager's Dilemma, by T.F. Carney (Time required: two and one-half to three hours.)

- To provide an opportunity to exchange views on the topic of delegation.

- To increase awareness of attitudes about task delegation.

('82-65)   **328. Reviewing Objectives and Strategies:** A Planning Task for Managers, by Cyril R. Mill (Time required: approximately three hours.)

- To review and evaluate an organization's accomplishments of the past year.

- To clarify and reaffirm the organizational mission.

- To prepare objectives and action steps for major organizational efforts in the next year.

('83-49)   **336. Vice President's In-Basket:** A Management Activity, by Annette N. Shelby (Time required: approximately three and one-half hours.)

- To focus attention on the issues involved in setting priorities for communication in organizations.

- To increase awareness of the role of delegation in organizations.

('86-55)   **421. Meeting Management:** Coping with Dysfunctional Behaviors, by Patrick Doyle and C.R. Tindal (Time required: approximately one hour for up to four groups. One and one-half hours for five or six groups.)

- To enable the participants to identify dysfunctional behaviors in meetings.

- To allow the participants to plan and test coping strategies for dealing with such behaviors in meetings.

('86-65)   **422. Raises:** Evaluating Employee Performance, by Allen J. Schuh (Time required: approximately two hours.)

- To provide participants with experience in considering qualifications for salary increases.

- To generate interest in and understanding of the importance and complexity of issues regarding salary increases.

('88-81)   **447. Delegation:** Using Time and Resources Effectively, by Michael N. O'Malley and Catherine M.T. Lombardozzi (Time required: approximately two hours and fifteen minutes.)

- To assist the participants in identifying barriers to delegation, the benefits of delegation, and which kinds of tasks can be delegated and which cannot.

- To present the participants with a method for delegating.

- To provide the participants with an opportunity to practice planning delegation in accordance with this method.

('89-89)   **459. The Robotics Decision:** Solving Strategic Problems, by Charles H. Smith (Time required: approximately three and one-half hours.)

- To introduce the participants to the strategic assumption surfacing and testing (SAST) process as a tool for solving complex strategic problems.

- To offer the participants an opportunity to use the SAST process in solving a sample problem.

('90-103)   **472. Termination:** Values and Decision Making, by Larry W. Sanders (Time required: one and one-half hours.)

- To offer the participants the opportunity to explore the impact of their values on individual and group decision making.

- To develop the participants' awareness of the need to identify objectives and to obtain sufficient information in group decision making.

- To provide the participants with an experience in group decision making.

('94-123)   **520. The Employment Case:** Exploring Organizational Value Conflicts, by Joann Keyton (Time required: one hour and twenty to thirty minutes.)

- To offer the participants an opportunity to examine, identify, and clarify their personal and professional values.

- To encourage the participants to explore the relationship between personal values and organizational values.

- To offer the participants an opportunity to influence and be influenced by one another in a value-based group decision-making task.

- To demonstrate how values affect organizational decision making.

- To reinforce the importance of making legal hiring decisions (by eliminating prejudice in hiring).

LEADERSHIP: Styles

(I-7)   **003. T-P Leadership Questionnaire:** An Assessment of Style (Time required: approximately forty-five minutes.)

- To evaluate oneself in terms of task orientation and people orientation.

(I-56)   **012. Choosing a Color:** A Multiple-Role-Play, by J. William Pfeiffer (Time required: approximately forty-five minutes.)

- To explore behavioral responses to an ambiguous task.

- To demonstrate the effects of shared leadership.

(II-58)   **035. Auction:** An Intergroup Competition, by J. William Pfeiffer (Time required: approximately one hour.)

- To explore relationships between leadership and decision making in a competitive situation.

- To illustrate effects of task success or failure on the selection of group representatives and leaders.

(IV-99)   **121. Toothpicks:** An Analysis of Helping Behaviors, by Ruth R. Middleman (Time required: approximately one hour.)

- To identify differing approaches to assisting others in a task.

- To explore the effects of the various helping approaches on task accomplishment and interpersonal relations.

(V-19)   **154. Styles of Leadership:** A Series of Role Plays, by Gerald M. Phillips (Time required: approximately two hours.)

- To explore the impact that leaders have on decision making in groups.

- To demonstrate the effects of hidden agendas.

(V-53)   **159. Fork-Labyrinth:** Leadership Practice, by John F. Veiga (Time required: approximately three hours.)

- To diagnose the behavior of leaders and followers in a small group performing a complex competitive task.

- To teach "on-line" feedback and coaching on leadership behavior.

- To practice different leadership behaviors.

(V-78)   **162. Pins and Straws:** Leadership Styles, by Howard L. Fromkin (Time required: approximately two hours.)

- To dramatize three general styles of leadership: autocratic, laissez-faire, and democratic.

- To increase awareness of how different styles of leadership can affect the performance of subordinates.

- To study the phenomenon of competition among groups.

('77-54)   **195. Executive Pie:** A Power Experience, by Stephan H. Putnam (Time required: approximately one hour.)

- To enhance the awareness of the uses of power in group decision making.

- To explore the values inherent in various styles of leadership.

- To simulate a common organizational problem.

(VI-39)   **207. Staff Meeting:** A Leadership Role Play, by Ernest M. Schuttenberg (Time required: approximately two and one-half hours. Additional time is required if lecturettes are presented.)

- To illustrate various styles of leadership and patterns of accommodation.

- To explore the effects of the interaction of leadership style and pattern of accommodation on individual motivation and decision making.

(VII-127)   **266. Power Personalities:** An OD Role Play, by Laura A. Jean, Jeffrey R. Pilgrim, Gary N. Powell, Deborah K. Stoltz, and Olivia S. White (Time required: approximately one and one-half to two hours.)

- To provide an opportunity to practice various power styles and behaviors.

- To learn which power-seeking tactics and bases of power are effective or ineffective in a problem-solving situation.

- To examine individual perceptions of and reactions to various power strategies.

('80-31)   **273. Managerial Characteristics:** Exploring Stereotypes, by Allen K. Gulezian (Time required: one and one-half to two hours.)

- To increase awareness of masculine and feminine characteristics typically associated with effective managerial performance.

- To examine the male-manager stereotype and its implications for women in management.

■ To provide an opportunity to examine self-perceptions relating to the concept of masculinity/femininity.

('80-37)   **274. Choosing an Apartment:** Authority Issues in Groups, by Julian J. Szucko, Richard L. Greenblatt, and Christopher B. Keys (Time required: two hours.)

■ To experience the impact of authoritarian behavior during a competitive activity.

■ To increase personal awareness of reactions to authoritarian behavior.

■ To experience the effects of hidden agendas on decision-making processes.

('80-54)   **277. Power and Affiliation:** A Role Play, by John F. Veiga and John N. Yanouzas (Time required: approximately one hour and forty-five minutes.)

■ To become better acquainted with positive and negative aspects of power and affiliation.

■ To explore the dynamics of power and affiliation in managerial situations.

(VIII-15)   **296. Boss Wanted:** Identifying Leadership Characteristics, by Graham L. Williams (Time required: approximately one and one-half hours.)

■ To allow individuals to examine their personal criteria for a good manager.

■ To compare preferences about managerial qualities.

■ To increase awareness of one's own current managerial strengths and weaknesses.

(VIII-108)   **313. Tangram:** Leadership Dimensions, by Eduardo Casais (Time required: approximately two hours.)

■ To identify key functions of a task-team leader.

- To examine the process of leading a team toward the accomplishment of a task.

- To experience the information-sharing process within a task team.

- To provide an opportunity to observe the effects of communication processes on members of a task team.

('83-19)   **331. Manager's Dilemma:** Theory X and Theory Y, by Rollin Glaser and Christine Glaser (Time required: approximately two and one-half hours.)

- To help participants to become aware of their own philosophies of human resource management.

- To introduce the concepts in McGregor's Theory X and Theory Y.

- To allow participants to compare and discuss alternative courses of action in a management situation.

(IX-31)   **346. Power Caucus:** Defining and Negotiating, by Bradford F. Spencer (Time required: one hour and forty-five minutes.)

- To help the participants to clarify their own definitions of power.

- To allow the participants to experience the similarities and differences between these definitions and the application of power in a real situation.

(IX-93)   **353. Management Skills:** Assessing Personal Performance, by Carol J. Levin (Time required: one hour and twenty-five minutes.)

- To heighten the participants' awareness of the wide range of behaviors that are encompassed by management.

- To enable the participants to assess their own needs for changes in their management-related behaviors.

('84-38)   **369. Follow the Leader:** An Introduction to Situational Leadership®, by Kaaren S. Brown and Donald M. Loppnow (Time required: approximately two and one-half hours.)

- To allow the participants to experience each of the four leadership styles that constitute the basis of Situational Leadership® theory.

- To explore the ways in which leadership styles, tasks, and work groups affect one another.

('85-45)   **381. Management Perspectives:** Identifying Styles, by Patrick Doyle (Time required: two hours and fifteen minutes.)

- To help the participants to identify various managerial styles.

- To illustrate the ways in which these managerial styles can affect an organization.

- To acquaint participants with the advantages and disadvantages of these styles.

('85-57)   **382. Chipping In:** Examining Management Strategies, by Kaaren Strauch-Brown (Time required: two hours and twenty minutes.)

- To demonstrate the effects of managerial behaviors on subordinates.

- To examine various communication strategies among managers and subordinates.

- To explore managers' use of resources in helping subordinates.

(X-85)   **401. Choose Me:** Developing Power Within a Group, by
Larry Porter (Time required: approximately two hours
and fifteen minutes.)

- To explore issues related to power and influence
  within a group.

- To offer each participant an opportunity to influence
  the other members of his or her group.

- To allow the participants to give and receive feedback
  about their personal approaches to developing power
  and influence within a group.

('87-69)   **433. Quantity Versus Quality:** Matching Perceptions of
Performance, by Allen J. Schuh (Time required: one to
one and one-half hours.)

- To enable managers to compare their perceptions with
  those of peers regarding the way each of them views
  the relative importance of quantity and quality in
  productivity.

- To help managers assess the accuracy and consistency
  of their individual perceptions by determining how
  closely they align with the perceptions of their peers.

('91-51)   **478. Rhetoric and Behavior:** Theory X and Theory Y, by
Maureen Vanterpool (Time required: two and one-half
hours.)

- To offer participants the opportunity to compare their
  managerial rhetoric with their behavior.

- To offer participants the opportunity to explore
  Theory X and Theory Y assumptions.

- To offer participants the opportunity to explore
  behaviors that demonstrate Theory X and Theory Y
  assumptions.

- To enable participants to set goals for self-monitored behavior changes and for using rhetoric and behavior that are consistent with Theory Y assumptions.

('92-37)   **488. The Good Leader:** Identifying Effective Behaviors, by Gerry Carline (Time required: approximately two hours and fifteen minutes.)

- To provide the participants with an opportunity to explore different view of leadership.

- To offer the participants an opportunity to discuss and identify the characteristics and behaviors that contribute to a leader's effectiveness.

- To encourage the participants to consider how leadership evolves in a group and the effects of various leadership behaviors on group members and task accomplishment.

('93-63)   **504. Organizational Structures:** A Simulation, by Rudi E. Weber (Time required: approximately two hours to two hours and fifteen minutes.)

- To assist participants in their efforts to understand the relationships between organizational structure, problem-solving performance, and organizational climate.

- To provide participants with an opportunity to experience and explore these relationships in a simulated environment.

- To encourage participants to examine the structures that prevail in their own work environments.

INTRODUCTION TO INVENTORIES, QUESTIONNAIRES, AND SURVEYS

Instrumented survey-feedback tools (generally inventories or measurement scales) can be used in a number of ways by group facilitators. Data from inventories can be interpreted normatively or intrapersonally, but it is important that they be coordinated carefully with the goals of the training design. Some uses of instrumentation include the following:

Providing instrumented feedback to group members. Participants complete, score, and interpret their own scales. They can be asked to predict one another's scores. They can fill out scales for one another as feedback.

Manipulating group composition. For brief, experimental demonstrations of the effects of group composition, various mixes of group members can be established. Long-term groups can be built that offer the promise of beneficial outcomes. Extremes of both homogeneity and heterogeneity can be avoided.

Teaching theory of interpersonal functioning. Some brief instruments are intended primarily to introduce concepts. Participants are involved with theory by investing in an activity such as completing an inventory related to the model being explored.

Researching outcomes of training interventions. Even scales with relatively low reliability can be effective in the study of group phenomena when used with pretest or follow-up procedures.

Studying here-and-now process in groups. It is sometimes helpful to use an instrument to assist the group in diagnosing its own internal functioning. The data can be focused on what is happening and what changes are desirable.

DISADVANTAGES AND ADVANTAGES OF USING INSTRUMENTS[1]

It is important to note both the advantages and the disadvantages of using instruments in training.

Disadvantages

One of the key disadvantages of using instruments is that people often fear that someone has, so to speak, obtained an indelible fingerprinting of them, that they have been exposed, that somebody has read their minds. It is important for facilitators using instruments to reduce this tendency to overstate the accuracy and stability of an instrument.

Another disadvantage is that instruments tend to encourage participants to be dependent on the facilitator, thus locating the leadership (control) of the group with the facilitator rather than allowing it to be shared among the members.

The use of instruments can be a means of dissipating the useful tension of person-to-person encounter, especially in a personal growth workshop. Both the participants and the leader may be denied some of the ambiguous but potentially growth-inducing tension produced by face-to-face encounter and reactions to one another.

Instruments often generate a rash of quarrelsome responses in which the participants question the items, reliability, validity, or relevance of an instrument. Much valuable time can be used in arguing about the instrument itself. This arguing often is a result of the fact that the participants have received information that disturbs them; they fear that their profiles *are* irrevocably descriptive of them or that people are going to interpret their data in a negative fashion.

Instruments also have the potential to generate significant hostility from participants who may see them as irrelevant, time consuming, and, in general, diverting attention from the key issues of the workshop.

---

[1] The following discussion on the disadvantages and advantages of using instruments is based on *Instrumentation in Human Relations Training* (2nd ed.) (pp. 11-17) by J.W. Pfeiffer, R. Heslin, and J.E. Jones, 1976, San Diego, CA: Pfeiffer & Company.

Finally, instruments can supply a person with more feedback than he or she is ready to handle; in other words, an instrument can overload participants with information that they do not have time to assimilate, to work through, to put into perspective.

Avoiding the Disadvantages

A number of the disadvantages mentioned can be avoided by removing the mysticism surrounding instruments. Effort should be made to prevent people from assuming that an instrument is an error-free opening of the soul to everyone. Rather, participants should be encouraged to view instrumented experiences like any other choice-making experience in their everyday lives. They have given answers to situations described in the instrument, added up those answers, and come up with scores. If they have trouble understanding where their scores came from, they should be encouraged to go back to each item fed into the score, examine how they responded to each item and how they scored it, and perhaps compare their responses to other people's—item by item, response by response, and situation by situation.

A second way to avoid some of the disadvantages of instruments is to make sure that individuals have sufficient time to process what the instrument has revealed about them. All participants should be given an opportunity to talk through their scores, to compare their scores in detail with those of others in the group, and to discuss why they see life from perspectives that are different from the perspectives of other participants. They may also discuss how their views of their scores reflect their personal orientations and may compare their views and orientations with those of other people.

Advantages

Instrumented approaches give the participants early opportunities to develop an understanding of the theories involved in the dynamics of their own group situations—understanding that will increase their involvement. By judiciously choosing an appropriate instrument during the first group session, the facilitator can quickly offer the participants a theory about personal styles or preferences, group or team development, interpersonal relations, or leadership that they can use throughout the rest of the group experience.

Another advantage of using instruments is that they give the participants some constructs and terminology early in the group experience that they can use in looking at their own and other people's behavior and in categorizing and describing what goes on between persons or within a person. A related advantage is that people form commitments to the information, constructs, and theory that they have been given, because their instrumented feedback describes them in terms of these constructs. One way of tying a person's ego to some useful theory about groups or interpersonal relations is to give the theory personal impact.

Another advantage is that participants can be given feedback about their personal behavior early in a group experience. In workshops participants often do not receive feedback about their styles or ways of relating to other participants until the last day, the last meeting, or the last two or three hours of the workshop. It may take that long before they have developed the skills necessary to give effective feedback and before an atmosphere of trust can be developed in the group so that members can feel comfortable in giving that kind of feedback to another member. Regardless of the causes of this situation, people then are faced with new information about themselves with no time to work on new behaviors that might modify those aspects described. Instruments administered early in the group experience help to compensate for the lack of feedback from others by giving each person some information about his or her style, perceptual framework toward other people, and reactions of others. Thus, people can generate agendas of behavior modification for themselves, based on the characteristics uncovered by the instrument, while they still have the remainder of the workshop to work on them.

Instruments surface latent issues that should be dealt with in the group setting. This is true whether the issues and problems are within an individual, between individuals, or within an organization. By administering an instrument that uncovers these issues, the facilitator makes these issues public, that is, outside the individual or the organization.

These issues then become legitimate materials to deal with, to discuss, to try to correct, or to improve.

Instruments give feedback to an individual or an organization in a way that is characterized by relatively low threat. When a person receives information from a questionnaire that he or she personally has filled out, the person is more likely to trust those data than data received from another individual about his or her personal style. At least the person does not have the dilemma of trying to sort out whether the information is mostly a function of his or her behavior, of the perceptual framework of the person who is giving the feedback, or of some chemistry that exists between the two of them. People can be fairly sure that the instrument holds no personal malevolence toward them; therefore, they can be freer to accept the information, understanding the fact that the information actually came from their own responses to descriptions of situations.

Another advantage is that instruments not only give individualized feedback about the respondents, but also allow the respondents to compare themselves with others. We all are aware that we may be more or less dominating than other people, that we may enjoy being with people more or less than others, that we may have a greater or lesser need for people to like us, and so on. However, it is often an eye-opening experience to find out that we are stronger in one or more of our characteristics than ninety-nine percent of the people in a certain norm group. This last piece of information, indicating that a person ranks not only high on a characteristic, but unusually high, may cause that person to pause and examine carefully whether this characteristic is becoming dysfunctional, for example, getting in the way of his or her performance on the job or at home.

Instruments allow the facilitator of a small group to focus the energies and time of the participants on the most appropriate material and also to control, to some extent, the matters that are dealt with in the workshop. In this way the facilitator is able to ensure that the issues worked on are crucial, existing ones rather than less important ones that the members may introduce to avoid grappling with the more uncomfortable issues.

A final advantage is that instruments allow longitudinal assessment of change in a group, an organization, or an individual. This assessment can be useful in organization development for demonstrating that the group interventions in which the organization is involved are compatible with the goals the consultant has determined from sensing efforts and/or compatible with the stated goals of the organization. This advantage is valuable in terms of group research and also for personal goal feedback.

SUMMARY

The Use of Instrumentation in Small Groups

Disadvantages

- Engenders fear of exposure
- Fosters dependency on the facilitator
- Relieves tension that could lead to growth
- Generates time-consuming nitpicking
- May be seen as diverting from key issues and may arouse hostility

Advantages

- Enables early, easy theoretical learning
- Develops early understanding of constructs and terminology
- Produces personal commitment to information, theory, and constructs
- Supplies early personal feedback
- Surfaces latent issues
- Allows facilitator to focus and control group appropriately
- Facilitates longitudinal assessment of change

Avoiding the Disadvantages of Instruments

1. The facilitator can make a concerted effort to remove the mysticism surrounding instrumentation:

   a. By discussing the margin of error and other factors that contribute to less-than-absolute results.

   b. By allowing and encouraging participants to explore the instrument thoroughly so that they see how it was designed and how their scores were derived.

   c. By showing participants how instrumentation is related to everyday, choice-making experiences.

2. The facilitator can ensure that sufficient time is made available for processing the data:

   a. By giving participants an opportunity to talk through their scores and to compare their scores with those of others.

   b. By emphasizing and legitimizing the differing life perspectives and orientations of people.

SEVEN PHASES IN USING AN INSTRUMENT

Using an instrument properly, that is, obtaining the best possible value from it, entails seven different phases: (1) administration, (2) theory input, (3) prediction, (4) scoring, (5) interpretation, (6) posting, and (7) processing.

In the first step, *administration*, a nonthreatening atmosphere should be established and the purposes of the instrument discussed. In larger groups, particularly, the administrator may need to tell those individuals who finish first to wait quietly for the others to finish.

Next, the facilitator should take a few minutes to give the participants some *theory input* for the instrument by explaining the rationale behind its use.

Each participant should be asked to make a *prediction* about his or her score(s) by estimating whether he or she will score high, medium, or low and by recording the estimate.

Scoring can be done in a number of ways. Some instruments require templates; some are self-scoring; and some require that scores be announced, written on newsprint, or handed out on a reproduced sheet. The sophistication of the particular group is a gauge of the most appropriate method of scoring. Sometimes it is more efficient for the facilitator or an assistant to do the scoring than to have participants do it. In this way, of course, individuals do not receive instant feedback, but often the instrument can be administered before a meal break and the results made available immediately after the break. The essential guideline in scoring is that it should not detract from the data being generated.

The manner in which *interpretation* is handled may vary widely, depending on the group and the style of the facilitator. One suggested way is to use two stages: (1) an interpretation of the administrator's (or another staff member's) scores, and then (2) an interpretation between pairs of participants. Thus, participants can first see how interpretations are made. Also, if staff members are willing to share their scores, participants find it less threatening to share theirs.

The sixth phase is *posting*. Displaying scores on newsprint can dissipate some people's concerns about possible negative values attached to their scores. At the same time, it can generate additional useful data for the group. Posting scores for discussion is particularly effective in subgroups.

The final, and perhaps most crucial, phase of instrumentation is *processing*. Group processing can simultaneously defuse negative affect and promote integration of the data concepts. Six to twelve participants form a group of ideal size for processing.

WHAT TO LOOK FOR IN AN INSTRUMENT

In examining the training applications and uses of instruments, we have identified some dimensions that need to be considered in selecting or assessing an instrument. The following chart reflects our judgment of the relative amount of concern each dimension warrants in training, organizational survey, personnel selection, and research applications.

INSTRUMENTATION APPLICATION

DIMENSION	Training	Organizational Assessment	Personnel Selection	Research
Validity* Are the data useful?	High	High	High	High
Reliability How accurate or stable are the scores?	Medium	Medium	Medium	High
Objectivity Is the scoring dependent on the judgments of the scorer, or is there a standard key?	High	High	High	Medium
Theoretical base Is the instrument based on a workable model?	High	High	Low	High
Behavorial orientation Are the scores derived from the respondents' descriptions of their behavior?	High	High	Low	Low
Observability Can the scores be related to the observable behavior of respondents?	High	Medium	Low	Low

---

*Validity takes on different meanings in these four contexts. In *training* the validity of the scale is in the user; that is, "Can I use this scale to help participants in training learn more effective behavior?" In *organizational assessment* the overriding consideration is "Does this instrument tap those process dimensions that are correlated with production?" In *personnel selection* the use of instruments centers around predictive—or discriminative—validity: "Is this instrument significantly related to a meaningful success criterion?" In *research* the major concern is the theoretical constructs being measured: "Does this scale measure the concepts derived from theory sufficiently well to permit meaningful tests of hypothesis derived from the model used?" Validity is always situation-specific; it resides not so much in the instrument as in the particular use of it.

INSTRUMENTATION APPLICATION

DIMENSION	Training	Organizational Assessment	Personnel Selection	Research
Language Is the instrument written at an appropriate reading level? Does it use a special vocabulary or jargon?	High	High	High	High
Special training How much professional preparation is required to use the scale?	High	High	High	High
Adaptability Can the items be adapted/ amended to fit a particular situation?	Medium	High	Low	Low
Copyright restrictions Can it be reprinted or edited without special permission?	High	Medium	Medium	Medium
Transparency How obvious is the rationale underlying the items?	Low	Low	High	Medium
Fakeability How easy is it for respondents to manipulate their scores?	Low	Medium	High	Medium
Norms Are relevant norms available?	Low	Low	High	Medium
Time required How much time is needed to prepare, administer, score, and interpret the instrument?	High	High	Low	Medium
Expense What is the cost of the materials, scoring, analyses, and background documents? Are these reusable materials?	Medium	High	Medium	Medium

INSTRUMENTATION APPLICATION

DIMENSION	Training	Organizational Assessment	Personnel Selection	Research
Accessibility Are the materials readily available?	Medium	Medium	Medium	Medium
Special materials Does the instrument require that any special apparatus be set up in advance?	High	Medium	Medium	Medium
Noxiousness Would the items—or the scale itself—offend intended respondents?	High	High	Medium	High
Scoring complexity Can the instrument be self-scored? Are electronic/clerical options available?	High	Low	Medium	Low
Data reduction How many scores are derived? Can these be summarized for ease in interpretation?	High	High	Medium	Low
Handouts Are easily read interpretive materials available to be distributed to respondents?	Medium	Medium	Low	Low
Familiarity How likely is it that participants will have responded to the scale before?	Low	Low	Medium	High

CLASSIFICATION OF INVENTORIES, QUESTIONNAIRES, AND SURVEYS

Since the publication of the 1984 *Annual,* the theoretical background necessary for understanding, presenting, and using each instrument has been included with the instrument, as well as all forms, scoring sheets, and interpretive materials. Thus, all the materials (including any pertinent lecturette material) that the facilitator needs in order to use an instrument from the 1984 *Annual* on are included either directly before or directly after the instrument form itself.

In this edition of the *Reference Guide,* we have reclassified the instruments to match the major categories used for experiential learning activities and presentation and discussion resources. Our intention is to help the user to find materials more quickly and with more discrimination. The instruments are classified according to what they measure—the focus of the information they provide—rather than according to how they might be used. The categories are as follows:

- Individual Development
- Communication
- Problem Solving
- Groups and Teams
- Consulting and Facilitating
- Leadership

INDIVIDUAL DEVELOPMENT

(II-103)   Life-Planning Program

('73-41)   Johari Window Self-Rating Sheet, by Philip G. Hanson

('73-89)   Involvement Inventory, by Richard Heslin and Brian
                Blake

(IV-110)   Risk-Taking Behavior in Groups Questionnaire, by
                Robert Kurtz

('74-104)   Self-Disclosure Questionnaire, by Sidney M. Jourard

('76-70)   Inventory of Self-Actualizing Characteristics (ISAC), by
                Anthony G. Banet, Jr.

('77-86)   Bem Sex-Role Inventory (BSRI), by Sandra Lipsitz Bem

('78-99)   Mach V Attitude Inventory, by Richard Christie

('79-88)   Satisfaction Survey: An Affective Personal Feedback
                Instrument, by Allen J. Schuh

(VII-150)   Sexual Values in Organizations Questionnaire, by Peggy
                Morrison and Richard DeGraw

('80-92)   Personal Style Inventory, by R. Craig Hogan and David
                W. Champagne

('82-102)   Life-Style Questionnaire, by Robert Driscoll and Daniel
                G. Eckstein

COMMUNICATION

('72-73)   Interpersonal Relationship Rating Scale, by John L. Hipple

('73-28)   Sex-Role Stereotyping Rating Scale, by Mary Carson

('73-55)   Helping Relationship Inventory, by John E. Jones

('73-73)   Scale of Feelings and Behavior of Love, by Clifford H. Swensen and Frank Gilner

('74-98)   Interpersonal Communication Inventory, by Millard J. Bienvenu, Sr.

('75-75)   Scale of Marriage Problems, by Clifford H. Swensen and Anthony Fiore

('76-81)   Inventory of Anger Communication (IAC), by Millard J. Bienvenu, Sr.

('76-105)   Organization Behavior Describer Survey (OBDS), by Roger Harrison and Barry Oshry

('77-91)   Interpersonal Check List (ICL), by Rolfe LaForge and Robert F. Suczek

('81-102)   Conflict-Management Climate Index, by Bob Crosby and John J. Scherer

('82-83)   Conflict-Management Style Survey, by Marc Robert

('84-115)   Communication Climate Inventory, by James I. Costigan and Martha A. Schmeidler

('84-126)   Styles Profile of Interaction Roles in Organizations
(SPIRO), by Udai Pareek

('86-104)   The Language System Diagnostic Instrument (LSDI), by
Cresencio Torres

('87-124)   Communication Congruence Inventory (CCI), by
Marshall Sashkin and Leonard D. Goodstein

('88-98)   Behavior Description, by John E. Oliver

PROBLEM SOLVING

(II-82)   Force-Field Analysis Inventory, based on Warren G.
Bennis and Saul Eisen

('75-83)   Problem-Analysis Questionnaire, by Barry Oshry and
Roger Harrison

('75-91)   Decision-Style Inventory, by Rick Roskin

('78-109)   Phases of Integrated Problem Solving (PIPS), by William
C. Morris and Marshall Sashkin

('83-126)   The TEM Survey: An Assessment of Your Effectiveness in
Managing Your Time, Energy, and Memory, by George J.
Petrello

('84-106)   Learning-Style Inventory, by Ronne Toker Jacobs and
Barbara Schneider Fuhrmann

('87-98)   Role Pics, by Udai Pareek

('89-123)   The Cognitive-Style Inventory, by Lorna P. Martin

('90-131)   Inventory of Barriers to Creative Thought and Innovative Action, by Lorna P. Martin

('92-135)   Locus of Control Inventory, by Udai Pareek

GROUPS AND TEAMS

(I-84)   Dependency-Intimacy Rating Form, by John E. Jones

(III-25)   Group-Climate Inventory

(III-26)   Group-Growth Evaluation Form

(III-30)   Postmeeting Reactions Form

(III-36)   Learning-Climate Analysis Form

(III-39)   Group-Behavior Questionnaire

(III-40)   Intentions and Choices Inventory

(III-76)   Team Building: Sensing Interview Guide

('72-91)   Group Leadership Questionnaire (GTQ-C), by Daniel B. Wile

CONSULTING AND FACILITATING

('78-226)   OD Readiness Check List, by J. William Pfeiffer and John E. Jones

('79-94)   Training Style Inventory (TSI), by Richard Brostrom

('79-102)   Power and OD Intervention Analysis (PODIA), by Marshall Sashkin and John E. Jones

('80-115)   Organizational Diagnosis Questionnaire (ODQ), by Robert C. Preziosi

('81-92)   Organizational-Process Survey, by Frank Burns and Robert L. Gragg

('82-91)   Survey of Program Participants, by Richard M. Wolf and W. Warner Burke

('82-98)   Follow-Up Survey of Program Participants, by Richard M. Wolf and W. Warner Burke

(IX-162)   Training Philosophies Profile, by G.E.H. Beamish

('86-81)   The Client-Consultant Questionnaire, by W. Warner Burke

('86-93)   Trainer Type Inventory (TTI), by Mardy Wheeler and Jeanie Marshall

('88-131)   Organizational-Learning Diagnostics (OLD), by Udai Pareek

('89-141)   The Organizational-Health Survey, by Will Phillips

('90-143)   The HRD Climate Survey, by T. Venkateswara Rao and
E. Abraham

('92-149)   Total Quality Management (TQM) Inventory, by Gaylord
Reagan

('93-123)   Consulting-Style Inventory, by Timothy M. Nolan

('93-155)   Empowerment-Readiness Survey, by April G. Henkel,
Cheryl Repp-Bégin, and Judith F. Vogt

('94-160)   Studying Organizational Ethos: The OCTAPACE Profile,
by Udai Pareek

('94-172)   Organizational-Type Inventory, by Manfred F.R. Kets de
Vries, Danny Miller, and Gaylord Reagan

LEADERSHIP

(I-10)   T-P Leadership Questionnaire, adapted from
Sergiovanni, Metzcus, and Burden

('72-67)   Supervisory Attitudes: The X-Y Scale

('72-79)   Intervention Style Survey, by B.H. Arbes

('73-44)   Motivation Feedback Opinionnaire, by Donald F.
Michalak

('73-97)   LEAD (Leadership: Employee-Orientation and
Differentiation) Questionnaire, by Russell Doré

('76-89)   Leader Effectiveness and Adaptability Description
             (LEAD), by Paul Hersey and Kenneth H. Blanchard

('79-82)   Women As Managers Scale (WAMS), by James R. Terborg

('81-98)   Supervisory Behavior Questionnaire, by Henry P. Sims, Jr.

(VIII-13)   People on the Job Work Sheet, by Martin B. Ross

(VIII-55)   When to Delegate Inventory Sheet, by T.F. Carney

('82-110)   Managerial Attitude Questionnaire, by Rick Roskin

('83-22)   Manager's Dilemma Work Sheet, by Rollin Glaser and
             Christine Glaser

('83-96)   Styles of Career Management, by Tom Carney

(IX-96)   Management Skills Inventory, by Carol J. Levin

('85-135)   The Entrepreneurial Orientation Inventory, by
             T. Venkateswara Rao

(X-130)   Sharing Perspectives Manager Sheet

(X-131)   Sharing Perspectives Worker Sheet

('86-118)   The Supervisory and Leadership Beliefs Questionnaire,
             by T. Venkateswara Rao

('86-121)   Motivational Analysis of Organizations—Behavior (MAO-B), by Udai Pareek

('87-115)   The Learning-Model Instrument, by Kenneth L. Murrell

('88-119)   The Visibility/Credibility Inventory, by W. Brendan Reddy and Gil Williams

('89-161)   Motivational Analysis of Organizations—Climate (MAO-C), by Udai Pareek

('91-163)   Managerial Work-Values Scale, by T. Venkateswara Rao

('91-179)   Management-Styles Spectrum, by Kenneth L. Murrell

('93-166)   Strategic Leadership Styles Instrument, by Gaylord Reagan

INTRODUCTION TO PRESENTATION AND DISCUSSION RESOURCES

USES OF PRESENTATION AND DISCUSSION RESOURCES

The presentation and discussion resources in the 1972 through 1994 *Annuals* open up a world of opportunity for a professional in the field of human resource development (HRD). These articles can be used as handouts or lecturette content for workshops, as sales tools, as personal learning tools, and as discussion starters.

Handouts or Lecturette Content

Many of the presentation and discussion resources make excellent handouts or sources of lecturette material. When planning training on a particular topic, the HRD practitioner may first determine goals and then look through the appropriate presentation and discussion resources for useful information to distribute to participants or to use as background material for a talk.

The lecturette is a highly effective method of focusing a participant's learning from an experiential learning activity or an intensive group meeting toward theoretical models. It can also provide a "cognitive map" for the experience that is to follow. It helps the participant transfer learning to everyday experiences by functioning as a guide to his or her behavior.

Even if a formal presentation is not desired, the practitioner may want to review the content of one or more articles on a topic so that he or she is well enough versed to lead a post-activity discussion in any desired direction. Also, during the course of a seminar or workshop, it often happens that one of the topics addressed strikes a participant's fancy. As a result, the participant asks the HRD practitioner for further information on the subject. When this happens, the practitioner may refer to the *Reference Guide* to locate appropriate information to satisfy the participant's needs.

Sales Tools

Often the concepts, theories, and practices of HRD are elusive to line managers and executives who were brought up on traditional principles of nonparticipative management. They may find these ideas completely foreign and may question the credibility of the HRD practitioner who introduces them. However, when the practitioner offers professionally written, edited, and produced articles that elucidate ideas in a straightforward manner, managers and executives may find such ideas not only more understandable but also more palatable.

The practitioner may use the presentation and discussion resources to explain a complex or subtle point, to document or support a particular position that he or she is recommending, or to illuminate the cloudy world of HRD technologies. Used in any of these ways, these articles enhance the HRD practitioner's credibility and simplify his or her job.

Professional Learning Tools

Becoming educated in the field of human resource development is no small undertaking. Especially for a new practitioner, the question of where to begin is not easy to answer. We believe that the presentation and discussion resources provide not just a useful starting point, but actually an entire education in HRD. All topics in the field are covered, from assumptions about the nature of human beings, to feedback, to risk taking, to assertion theory, to conflict and stress, to negotiation, to defensive and supportive communication, to poor listening habits, to face-to-face selling for consultants, to complex issues related to management or organization development or the design of training programs.

In addition, because Pfeiffer & Company has been publishing articles in HRD virtually since the inception of the field, these articles represent the history of the field and can be used to trace developments over time.

Discussion Starters

Many aspects of an HRD practitioner's professional life are exciting, but few are more lively or stimulating than discussions about issues in the field with fellow practitioners. Such discussions represent one of the practitioner's best sources of learning; through them he or she can test the practicality of ideas, disseminate information and receive information in return, and reap the benefits of another's experience and expertise. In these discussions fellow professionals can serve as coaches and mentors for one another.

Sharing the presentation and discussion resources with fellow practitioners can bring the information to life. There is no better way to build collegiality while enhancing knowledge of the field.

CLASSIFICATION OF PRESENTATION AND DISCUSSION RESOURCES

In the 1984 *Annual,* we introduced the "Professional Development" section, which includes the type of contents previously found in the Lecturettes, Theory and Practice, and Resources sections of the 1972-1983 *Annuals.* This allowed us more flexibility in integrating information—expository text with a bibliography, for example—and more accurately describes the purpose of the articles, listings, and other material that appear in this section. In the 1994 *Annual,* this section was renamed "Presentation and Discussion Resources." Beginning with the 1994 *Reference Guide,* the "Presentation and Discussion Resources" section combines all of the materials that were previously indexed separately. All of the materials that have been categorized as "Lecturettes," "Theory and Practice," "Resources," "Professional Development," or "Presentation and Discussion Resources" are now compiled in one section in the following categories and subcategories:

- Individual Development
  - Developing Awareness and Understanding
  - Personal Growth
  - Life/Career Planning
  - Change and Risk Taking
  - Stress and Burnout
- Communication
  - Clarity and Precision in Communication
  - Communication Styles, Modes, and Patterns
  - Feedback
  - Coaching and Encouraging
  - Confrontation and Negotiation
  - Communication in Organizations

- Problem Solving
  - Models, Methods, and Techniques
  - Competition, Collaboration, and Negotiation
  - Conflict
  - Change and Change Agents

- Groups and Teams
  - Types of Groups
  - Group Process
  - Behavior and Roles in Groups
  - Group Development
  - Team Building and Team Development
  - Techniques To Use with Groups

- Consulting
  - Organizations: Their Characteristics and How They Function
  - OD Theory and Practice
  - Consulting Strategies and Techniques
  - Interface with Clients

- Facilitating
  - Theories and Models of Facilitating
  - Techniques and Strategies
  - Evaluation

- Leadership
  - Theories and Models
  - Strategies and Techniques
  - Top-Management Issues and Concerns

INDIVIDUAL DEVELOPMENT:
Developing Awareness and Understanding

('72-119)   Assumptions About the Nature of Man, by John E. Jones

('72-125)   The Maslow Need Hierarchy, by Sandra L. Pfeiffer

('73-132)   Dependency and Intimacy, by John E. Jones

('73-203)   Some Implications of Value Clarification for Organization Development, by Maury Smith

('74-131)   Figure/Ground, by Judith James Pfeiffer

('75-123)   Human Needs and Behavior, by Anthony J. Reilly

('75-132)   Open Systems, by David J. Marion

('75-183)   A Gestalt Primer, by J. William Pfeiffer and Judith A. Pfeiffer

('75-238)   Awareness Through Movement, by Moshe Feldenkrais

('76-120)   The Awareness Wheel, by Sherod Miller, Elam W. Nunnally, and David B. Wackman

('76-139)   Power, by Dennis C. King and John C. Glidewell

('76-143)   Alternatives to Theorizing, by Stanley M. Herman

('76-274)   Values Clarification: A Review of Major Books, by Joel Goodman

('93-181)   The Dunn and Dunn Model of Learning Styles: Addressing Learner Diversity, by Joanne Ingham and Rita Dunn

('94-121)   Disability Awareness Background Sheet, by Robert William Lucas

INDIVIDUAL DEVELOPMENT: Personal Growth

('75-141)   Therapy or Personal Growth?, by Timothy A. Boone

('75-241)   An Introduction to Structural Integration (Rolfing), by Roger Pierce

('75-246)   What Is Psychosynthesis?

('76-211)   Interrole Exploration, by Udai Pareek

('76-235)   Bioenergetic Therapy, by Philip Katz

('76-238)   Hatha Yoga, by Lorrie Collins Trueblood

('77-99)   Centering, by Anthony G. Banet, Jr.

('77-102)   Androgyny, by Jean Campbell

('78-170)   Personal Effectiveness, by Udai Pareek

('79-113)   How To Maintain Personal Energy, by John E. Jones

('79-133)   The Centered Boss, by Peter Scholtes

('80-138)   Jealousy: A Proactive Approach, by Colleen Kelley

('80-143)   Dimensions of Role Efficacy, by Udai Pareek

('80-175)   Methods of Centering, by Anthony G. Banet, Jr.

('81-141)   Intrapersonal Conflict Resolution, by Hugh Pates

('83-273)   Biofeedback: An Outline of the Literature and Resource
Directory (1983 Update), by Howard Pikoff

('85-141)   The Support Model, by Juliann Spoth, Barry H. Morris,
and Toni C. Denton

('86-201)   Developing and Increasing Role Efficacy, by Udai Pareek

('88-35)   Creating Ideal Personal Futures: The Nature of Personal
Premises, by John D. Adams

INDIVIDUAL DEVELOPMENT: Life/Career Planning

('72-141)   The International Association of Applied Social
Scientists, by Kenneth D. Benne and Steven J. Ruma

('72-231)   Alphabet Soup, by Frank Johnson

('73-267)   Growth Centers, by William Swartley

('74-189)   Life/Work Planning, by Art Kirn and Marie Kirn

('74-215)   Individual Needs and Organizational Goals: An
Experiential Lecture, by Anthony J. Reilly

('74-255)   AHP Growth Center List, by Association for Humanistic Psychology

('75-249)   Applied Behavioral Science Consulting Organizations: A Directory

('77-252)   AHP Growth Center List, 1976, by Association for Humanistic Psychology

('78-229)   Graduate Programs in Applied Behavioral Science: A Directory, by Susan Campbell

('79-270)   AHP Growth Center List, 1978

('80-152)   Job-Related Adaptive Skills: Toward Personal Growth, by John J. Scherer

('80-265)   Alphabet Soup: 1980, by Frank Pierce Johnson

('80-271)   Applied Behavioral Science Consulting Organizations: An Updated Directory

('80-285)   Career Development: Literature and Resources, by Howard L. Fromkin and James D. McDonald

('82-217)   Growth Center Directory: 1982 Update

('82-231)   Graduate Programs in Applied Behavioral Science: An Updated Directory

('83-255)   Applied Behavioral Science Consulting Organizations: An Updated Directory

('83-282)   Executive Recruiters: A Directory, by Leslie Whitaker

INDIVIDUAL DEVELOPMENT: Change and Risk Taking

('74-148)   Personal and Organizational Pain: Costs and Profits, by
             Philip J. Runkel

('78-143)   The Pendulum Swing: A Necessary Evil in the Growth
             Cycle, by Beverly A. Gaw

('79-117)   The Emotional Cycle of Change, by Don Kelley and Daryl
             R. Conner

('89-211)   Creative Risk Taking, by Richard E. Byrd and Jacqueline
             L. Byrd

('90-171)   Overcoming Mind Traps: Self-Change and Its
             Implications for the HRD Professional, by Tom Rusk

INDIVIDUAL DEVELOPMENT: Stress and Burnout

('77-143)   Consultant Burnout, by Michael D. Mitchell

('81-138)   Stress-Management Skills: Self-Modification for Personal
             Adjustment to Stress, by L. Phillip K. Le Gras

('83-175)   Surviving Organizational Burnout, by John M. Shearer

('85-42)   Gaining Support Theory Sheet, by Juliann Spoth, Barry
             H. Morris, and Toni C. Denton

(X-103)   Sticky Wickets Group-Stress Theory Sheet, by William B.
             Kline and Joseph J. Blase

('93-291)   Stress-Management Training for the Nineties, by Beverly
             Byrum-Robinson

COMMUNICATION:
Clarity and Precision in Communication

('73-120)   Conditions Which Hinder Effective Communication, by J. William Pfeiffer

('73-139)   Thinking and Feeling, by Anthony G. Banet, Jr.

('74-203)   "Don't You Think That...?": An Experiential Lecture on Indirect and Direct Communication, by J. William Pfeiffer and John E. Jones

('75-115)   Humanistic Numbers, by John E. Jones

('76-149)   Clarity of Expression in Interpersonal Communication, by Myron R. Chartier

('78-119)   Communication Effectiveness: Active Listening and Sending Feeling Messages, by Jack N. Wismer

('81-124)   Kenepathy, by Michele Stimac

(X-65)   Taking Responsibility Theory Sheet, by Gilles L. Talbot

('88-41)   E-Prime Theory Sheet, by Gilles L. Talbot

COMMUNICATION:
Communication Styles, Modes, and Patterns

('72-173)   Communication Modes: An Experiential Lecture, by John E. Jones

(’73-145)   A Transactional Analysis Primer, by John P. Anderson

(’74-129)   Making Requests Through Metacommunication, by
              Charles M. Rossiter, Jr.

(’75-155)   Nonverbal Communication and the Intercultural
              Encounter, by Melvin Schnapper

(’77-147)   Toward Androgynous Trainers, by Melinda S. Sprague
              and Alice Sargent

(’77-227)   A Bibliography of Nonverbal Communication, by Robert
              W. Rasberry

(’78-123)   Communicating Communication, by J. Ryck Luthi

(’79-128)   Anybody with Eyes Can See the Facts!, by Aharon
              Kuperman

(’80-127)   The Four-Communication-Styles Approach, by Tom Carney

(’82-159)   Jargon: Rediscovering a Powerful Tool, by Lilith Ren

(’82-166)   Understanding and Improving Communication
              Effectiveness, by Gustave J. Rath and Karen S. Stoyanoff

(’86-213)   A Primer on Social Styles, by Beverly Byrum

(’87-29)   Poor Listening Habits Theory Sheet, by Joseph Seltzer
              and Leland W. Howe

COMMUNICATION: Feedback

COMMUNICATION: Coaching and Encouraging

COMMUNICATION: Confrontation and Negotiation

COMMUNICATION: Communication in Organizations

('79-194)   The Behavioral Science Roots of Organization
            Development: An Integrated Perspective, by Thomas H.
            Patten, Jr.

('87-151)   Competence in Managing Lateral Relations, by
            W. Warner Burke and Celeste A. Coruzzi

('88-179)   Designing More Effective Orientation Programs, by
            Daniel C. Feldman

('89-34)   What's Legal? Clarification Sheet, by Robert J. ("Jack")
            Cantwell

('90-281)   Legendary Customer Service and the HRD Professional's
            Role, by Gary M. Heil and Richard W. Tate

('91-32)   Quality Customer Service Idea Sheet, by Bonnie Jameson

('93-193)   How To Make New-Employee Orientation a Success, by
            Jean Barbazette

('93-247)   Sexual Differences in the Workplace: The Need for
            Training, by Arlette C. Ballew and Pamela Adams-Regan

PROBLEM SOLVING: Models, Methods, and Techniques

('72-135)   An Introduction to PERT...or..., by D.E. Yoes

('73-111)   Kurt Lewin's "Force-Field Analysis," by Morris S. Spier

('74-125)   Five Components Contributing to Effective Interpersonal
            Communications, by Myron R. Chartier

('93-17) Career Visioning Theory Sheet, by Neil Johnson and Jason Ollander-Krane

PROBLEM SOLVING:
Competition, Collaboration, and Negotiation

('73-105) Win/Lose Situations, by Gerry E. Wiley

('73-195) Planned Renegotiation: A Norm-Setting OD Intervention, by John J. Sherwood and John C. Glidewell

('76-203) A Gestalt Approach to Collaboration in Organizations, by H.B. Karp

('81-165) Developing Collaboration in Organizations, by Udai Pareek

('91-199) Negotiation Today: Everyone Wins, by Beverly Byrum-Robinson

PROBLEM SOLVING: Conflict

('74-139) Conflict-Resolution Strategies, by Joan A. Stepsis

('77-115) Constructive Conflict in Discussions: Learning To Manage Disagreements Effectively, by Julia T. Wood

('77-120) Handling Group and Organizational Conflict, by Donald T. Simpson

PROBLEM SOLVING: Change and Change Agents

GROUPS AND TEAMS: Types of Groups

('83-157)   A Look at Quality Circles, by H.B. Karp

('88-201)   Quality Circles: After the Honeymoon, by Edward E. Lawler III and Susan A. Mohrman

('88-215)   Outstanding Performance Through Superteams, by Julia Pokora and Wendy Briner

GROUPS AND TEAMS: Group Process

('74-179)   Therapeutic Intervention and the Perception of Process, by Anthony G. Banet, Jr.

('80-133)   Interaction Process Analysis, by Beverly Byrum-Gaw

('82-128)   Major Growth Processes in Groups, by John E. Jones

('82-190)   Group Process Demystified, by Robert L. Burton

('92-185)   Group Size as a Function of Trust, by Patrick Leone

GROUPS AND TEAMS: Behavior and Roles in Groups

('72-109)   Guidelines for Group Member Behavior, by J. William Pfeiffer

('72-117)   Defense Mechanisms in Groups, by Paul Thoresen

('72-179)   Transcendence Theory, by J. William Pfeiffer

('73-108)   Synergy and Consensus Seeking, by John E. Jones

GROUPS AND TEAMS: Group Development

('72-157)   TORI Theory and Practice, by Jack R. Gibb

('73-127)   A Model of Group Development, by John E. Jones

('74-142)   Cog's Ladder: A Model of Group Development, by
George O. Charrier

('76-169)   Yin/Yang: A Perspective on Theories of Group
Development, by Anthony G. Banet, Jr.

('80-182)   Accelerating the Stages of Group Development, by John
J. Scherer

('82-124)   Stages of Group Development, by Peter P. Fay and Austin
G. Doyle

('82-140)   Issues Present When Entering a System, by Richard
Hensley

('82-198)   Group Energy, Group Stage, and Leader Interventions,
by C. Jesse Carlock and Beverly Byrum-Gaw

('85-217)   A Situational Leadership®Approach to Groups Using the
Tuckman Model of Group Development, by Chuck
Kormanski

('94-213)   Fostering the Effectiveness of Groups at Work, by Patrick
J. Ward and Robert C. Preziosi

GROUPS AND TEAMS:
Team Building and Team Development

('74-227) Team Building, by Anthony J. Reilly and John E. Jones

('77-181) Team Development: A Training Approach, by Lawrence N. Solomon

('80-157) Team Building from a Gestalt Perspective, by H.B. Karp

('83-267) Team Building/Team Development: A Reference List, by Richard C. Diedrich

('85-101) The Team Effectiveness Critique, by Mark Alexander

('87-255) A New Model of Team Building: A Technology for Today and Tomorrow, by Chuck Kormanski and Andrew Mozenter

GROUPS AND TEAMS: Techniques To Use with Groups

('72-185) Contracts in Encounter Groups, by Gerard Egan

('74-197) Cybernetic Sessions: A Technique for Gathering Ideas, by John T. Hall and Roger A. Dixon

('75-111) Common Problems in Volunteer Groups, by Ed Bancroft

('77-155) A Tavistock Primer, by Anthony G. Banet, Jr. and Charla Hayden

('79-174)   The Delphi Technique: A Projection Tool for Serious Inquiry, by Richard L. Bunning

('80-199)   Videotape Techniques for Small Training Groups, by Jerry L. Fryrear

('81-183)   Meeting Management, by David R. Nicoll

('82-121)   A Structured Format for Improving Meetings, by Jack J. Rosenblum

('83-145)   Toward More Effective Meetings, by Mike M. Milstein

('83-203)   Video-Enhanced Human Relations Training: Self-Modeling and Behavior Rehearsal in Groups, by Jerry L. Fryrear and Stephen A. Schneider

CONSULTING: Organizations: Their Characteristics and How They Function

('73-130)   Three Approaches to Organizational Learning, by Anthony J. Reilly

('75-126)   Skill Climate and Organizational Blockages, by David L. Francis

('75-199)   Understanding Your Organization's Character, by Roger Harrison

('75-211)   Dimensions of the Organizational Universe: A Model for Assessment and Direction, by David J. Marion

('77-123)   Organizational Norms, by Mark Alexander

CONSULTING: OD Theory and Practice

('76-225)   A Current Assessment of OD: What It Is and Why It Often Fails, by J. William Pfeiffer and John E. Jones

('76-241)   A Reference List for Change Agents, by Larry E. Pate

('77-209)   Constructive Citizen Participation, by Desmond M. Connor

('77-217)   Ethical Considerations in Consulting, by J. William Pfeiffer and John E. Jones

('77-276)   Organization Development: A Review of Recent Books (1973-1976), by Marshall Sashkin

('78-219)   OD Readiness, by J. William Pfeiffer and John E. Jones

('80-249)   A Brief Glossary of Frequently Used Terms in Organization Development and Planned Change, by Marshall Sashkin

('81-259)   Periodicals in Organization Development and Related Fields, by Steven M. Rosenthal and L. Paul Church

('82-150)   An OD Flow Chart: From Beginning to End, by William A. Gamble

('82-208)   Holistic Human Resource Development: Beyond Techniques and Procedures, by Roger Kaufman

('83-241)   Organizational Analysis, Design, and Implementation: An Approach for Improving Effectiveness, by David A. Nadler

('84-155)   Human Resource Development: Current Status and Future Directions, by Leonard D. Goodstein and J. William Pfeiffer

('84-176)   Organizational Use of the Behavioral Sciences: The Improbable Task, by Warren Bennis

('84-207)   An Organization Development (OD) Primer, by Leonard D. Goodstein and Phyliss Cooke

('85-227)   Integrated Human Resource Development Systems, by T. Venkateswara Rao

('86-145)   Similarities and Differences Between Internal and External Consulting, by Lynda C. McDermott

('86-177)   Human Resource Development in a Changing World, by Gordon L. Lippitt

('86-239)   Structuring the OD Function in Corporate America, by Barbara Benedict Bunker

('86-249)   Organization Development Resource Guide: A Bibliography, by Homer H. Johnson

('87-169)   Toward Functional Organizational Development: What To Do After the Search and the Passion for Excellence, by Roger Kaufman

('88-189)   Organization Development: The Evolution to "Excellence" and Corporate Culture, by Thomas H. Patten, Jr.

('88-223)   The Conference As Context for Implementing Organizational-Improvement Strategies, by L. D. Terry

('89-267)   Model A: A Design, Assessment, and Facilitation Template in the Pursuit of Excellence, by Gerard Egan

('90-209)   Characteristics of Successful Organization Development: A Review of the Literature, by Peggy G. Walters

('92-223)   An Annotated Bibliography on the Work Force of the Twenty-First Century: Baby Boom and Bust, by Mary Ellen Collins

('93-72)   Organizational Structures Background Sheet, by Rudi E. Weber

('93-83)   The Hundredth Monkey Theory Sheet, by Marian K. Prokop

CONSULTING: Consulting Strategies and Techniques

('72-211)   Notes on Freedom, by Stanley M. Herman

('77-129)   Consulting Process in Action, by Ronald Lippitt and Gordon L. Lippitt

('77-195)   Intervening in Organizations Through Reward Systems, by Thomas H. Patten, Jr.

('78-133)   Strategies for Designing an Intervention, by Glenn H. Varney

('80-213)   Consultation to Human-Service Organizations, by Leonard D. Goodstein

CONSULTING: Interface with Clients

('91-225)   Face-to-Face Selling for Consultants, by Don M. Schrello

('93-221)   The Initial Interview: Assessing Client Needs, by Dan Stone and Robert J. Marshak

FACILITATING: Theories and Models of Facilitating

('72-203)   The Concept of Structure in Experiential Learning, by Ruth R. Middleman and Gale Goldberg

('73-159)   Hill Interaction Matrix (HIM) Conceptual Framework for Understanding Groups, by Wm. Fawcett Hill

('73-177)   Design Considerations in Laboratory Education, by J. William Pfeiffer and John E. Jones

('73-225)   A Two-Phase Approach to Human Relations Training, by Gerard Egan

('73-247)   A Personalized Human Relations Training Bibliography, by Maury Smith

('74-155)   The Message from Research, by Jack R. Gibb

('75-161)   The Experiential Learning Model and Its Application to Large Groups, by Stephen E. Marks and William L. Davis

('75-167)   Structured Experiences in Groups: A Theoretical and Research Discussion, by Robert R. Kurtz

('75-264)   A Bibliography of Small-Group Training, 1973-1974, by W. Brendan Reddy

('76-265)   Humanistic Education: A Review of Books Since 1970, by Patricia A. Schmuck and Richard A. Schmuck

('76-280)   Transactional Analysis: A Review of the Literature, by Hedges Capers

('77-238)   A Bibliography of Small-Group Training, 1974-1976, by W. Brendan Reddy and Kathy Lippert

('78-277)   Humanistic and Transpersonal Education: A Guide to Resources, by Jack Canfield

('81-284)   A Bibliography of Small-Group Training, 1976-1979, by W. Brendan Reddy and Kathy M. Lippert

('82-266)   An Annotated Bibliography and Critique of Reviews of Group Research, by Rex Stockton

('83-187)   Modeling: Teaching by Living the Theory, by Beverly Byrum-Gaw and C. Jesse Carlock

('83-223)   A Model for Training Design: Selecting Appropriate Methods, by Donald T. Simpson

('84-257)   The Expectancy Theory of Motivation: Implications for Training and Development, by John A. Sample

('86-137)   The HRD Professional: Master of Many Roles, by Tom W. Goad

('87-269)   Thirty Years of Human Service Education and Training—One Perspective, by Hedley G. Dimock

('93-113)   Zodiac for Trainers Theory Sheet, by Bonnie Jameson

('94-273)   Theme Development: Finally Getting Control of the Design Process, by H.B. Karp

FACILITATING: Techniques and Strategies

('72-225)   Counseling and Clinical Training Applications of Human Relations Theory and Practice, by Richard Levin

('72-235)   Games and Simulations: Materials, Sources, and Learning Concepts, by Brent D. Ruben

('72-241)   Media Resources for Human Relations Training, by Norman Felsenthal

('74-249)   Human Relations Training in the UK and Continental Europe, by Cary L. Cooper

('75-129)   Re-Entry, by John E. Jones

('75-138)   Training Components for Group Facilitators, by Robert K. Conyne

('75-219)   Co-Facilitating, by J. William Pfeiffer and John E. Jones

('75-233)   Canada's Experience with Human Relations Training, by Hedley G. Dimock

('76-157)   Designing and Facilitating Experiential Group Activities: Variables and Issues, by Cary L. Cooper and Kenneth Harrison

('76-185)   Working with Couples: Some Basic Considerations, by Herbert A. Otto

('83-195)   Dance/Movement Therapy: A Primer for Group Facilitators, by Susan Frieder Wallock and Daniel G. Eckstein

('84-195)   Needs Assessment: Avoiding the "Hammer" Approach, by Joe Thomas

('85-147)   The Use of the Training Contract, by H.B. Karp

('85-155)   Videotapes and Vicarious Learning: A Technology for Effective Training, by Dennis A. Gioia and Henry P. Sims, Jr.

('87-203)   Diagnosing the Training Situation: Matching Instructional Techniques with Learning Outcomes and Environment, by Carol Rocklin Kay, Sue Kruse Peyton, and Robert Pike

('87-213)   Forecasting the Economic Benefits of Training, by Richard A. Swanson and Gary D. Geroy

('89-183)   New Age Training Technologies: The Best and the Safest, by Beverly Byrum

('90-191)   Needs Assessment: Forerunner to Successful HRD Programs, by Allison Rossett

('92-115)   Up Close and Personal with Dr. Maslow Theory Sheet, by Bonnie Jameson

('92-117)   Up Close and Personal with Dr. Maslow Resource Sheet, by Bonnie Jameson

('93-213)   The Effective Use of Humor in Human Resource
Development, by Ozzie Dean

FACILITATING: Evaluation

('80-224)   Evaluation of Human-Service Programs, by Karen Sue
Trisko and V.C. League

('89-223)   Evaluation: Issues First, Methodology Second, by Phyliss
Cooke and Ralph R. Bates

('91-245)   Basic Statistics for the HRD Practitioner, by Joseph J.
Maiorca

('91-267)   A Matrix for Evaluating Training, by Jeanette Goodstein
and Leonard D. Goodstein

('91-287)   Evaluation and Management Development, by Nancy M.
Dixon

('94-279)   Evaluating the Effectiveness of Training Programs, by
Patricia E. Boverie, Deanna Sánchez Mulcahy, and John
A. Zondlo

LEADERSHIP: Theories and Models

('72-121)   McGregor's Theory X-Theory Y Model, by Albert J.
Robinson

('72-130)   Management by Objectives, by Thomas M. Thomson

('75-120)   Participatory Management: A New Morality, by Joan A. Stepsis

('75-195)   The White Paper: A Tool for OD, by Thomas H. Patten, Jr.

('76-132)   Leadership as Persuasion and Adaptation, by Julia T. Wood

('77-110)   A Practical Leadership Paradigm, by Timothy A. Boone

('81-206)   An Overview of Ten Management and Organizational Theorists, by Marshall Sashkin

('84-145)   A Bibliography of Applications of the Myers-Briggs Type Indicator (MBTI) to Management and Organizational Behavior, by John A. Sample

('84-161)   Line Managers and Human Resource Development, by Udai Pareek and T. Venkateswara Rao

('84-168)   OD with a Management Perspective, by John C. Lewis

('84-216)   Sociotechnical Systems Thinking in Management Consulting: A Holistic Concept for Organization Development, by Arthur Zobrist and Robert E. Enggist

('85-53)   Management Perspectives Theory Sheet, by Patrick Doyle

('86-69)   Raises Theory Sheet, by Allen J. Schuh

('87-157)   Impact at Ground Zero: Where Theory Meets Practice, by Patrick Doyle and C.R. Tindal

LEADERSHIP: Strategies and Techniques

('88-84)   Delegation Theory Sheet, by Michael N. O'Malley and
Catherine M.T. Lombardozzi

('88-229)   Applying a Consulting Model to Managerial Behavior, by
Terry Newell

('89-42)   Four Factors Theory Sheet, by William N. Parker

('90-225)   Sexual Harassment of Women in the Workplace:
Managerial Strategies for Understanding, Preventing,
and Limiting Liability, by Joyce Lynn Carbonell, Jeffrey
Higginbotham, and John Sample

('90-249)   Performance Coaching, by Udai Pareek and
T. Venkateswara Rao

('92-213)   From Controlling to Facilitating: How To L.E.A.D., by
Fran Rees

('92-241)   Managing Diversity in the Workplace, by S. Kanu Kogod

('93-201)   Managing and Motivating the Culturally Diverse Work
Force, by Sondra Thiederman

('94-130)   The Employment Case Theory Sheet, by Joann Keyton

('94-189)   Danger—Diversity Training Ahead: Addressing the Myths
of Diversity Training and Offering Alternatives, by Paula
Grace

('94-201)   Behavior-Management Interventions: Getting the Most
Out of Your Employee Assistance Program, by Robert T.
Brill

LEADERSHIP: Top-Management Issues and Concerns

('74-146)   The "Shouldist" Manager, by Stanley M. Herman

('83-231)   Managing Supervisory Transition, by Raymond J. Zugel

('84-227)   A Guide to Participative Management, by Marshall Sashkin

('84-242)   The Transformational Manager: Facilitating the Flow State, by Linda S. Ackerman

('85-275)   Applied Strategic Planning: A New Model for Organizational Growth and Vitality, by Leonard D. Goodstein, J. William Pfeiffer, and Timothy M. Nolan

('87-179)   Why Employee Involvement Often Fails and What It Takes To Succeed, by Bob Crosby

('87-197)   Humanizing the Work Place, by Eva Schindler-Rainman

('88-54)   Four Corners Theory Sheet, by Bonnie Jameson

('88-255)   Strategies for Helping Managers to Downsize Organizations, by Lynda C. McDermott

('89-241)   Fostering Intrapreneurship in Organizations, by Gifford Pinchot III

('89-255)   A Model for the Executive Management of Transformational Change, by Richard Beckhard

('90-32)   Words Apart Theory Sheet, by Mark Maier

('90-265)   Linking Strategic Planning to the Management of People, by Michael C. Busch

('92-84)   Working at Our Company Theory Sheet, by Leonard D. Goodstein

('92-251)   Time-Based Evolution and Faster Cycle Time, by Kenneth W. Herzog

('93-231)   Growing by Leaps and Bounds: Management Development Through Key Growth Experiences, by Jason Ollander-Krane and Neil Johnson

NAME INDEX

TITLE INDEX

Editorial

Dawn Kilgore, Project Manager
Susan Rachmeler
Marian K. Prokop
Carol Nolde

Graphics and Page Composition

Judy Whalen, Project Manager
Lee Ann Hubbard

This book was edited and formatted using 486 platforms with 8MB RAM and high-resolution, dual-page monitors. The copy was produced using WordPerfect software; pages composed with Ventura software; and illustrations produced in CorelDraw. The text is set in eleven on thirteen New Baskerville and the heads are Panache Bold. Camera-ready copy was output on a 1200-dpi laser imagesetter by Pfeiffer & Company.